Mastering

IntelliJ IDEA

Unlock Your Coding Potential with Advanced Techniques and Best Practices

Table to content

CHAPTER 10: MASTERING INTELLIJ IDEA 171

Chapter 1: Introduction to IntelliJ IDEA

1.1 What is IntelliJ IDEA?

IntelliJ IDEA is a robust and feature-rich integrated development environment (IDE) developed by JetBrains. Primarily designed for Java development, IntelliJ IDEA has evolved into a versatile IDE that supports a broad range of programming languages, including Kotlin, Groovy, Scala, and even JavaScript, TypeScript, and various other languages through plugins. IntelliJ IDEA's powerful set of tools and intuitive user interface make it a preferred choice for developers who aim to enhance their productivity and code quality.

Overview of IntelliJ IDEA

IntelliJ IDEA stands out among IDEs due to its focus on developer ergonomics. It offers a blend of advanced features such as intelligent code completion, on-the-fly code analysis, and powerful refactoring tools. These features enable developers to write, debug, and maintain code more efficiently.

Key features of IntelliJ IDEA include:

- **Intelligent Code Completion**: IntelliJ IDEA offers context-aware code completion, which not only suggests class names and methods but also understands the scope and context to provide the most relevant suggestions.
- **On-the-Fly Code Analysis**: The IDE continuously monitors your code for potential errors and warnings, providing immediate feedback to help maintain code quality.
- **Refactoring Tools**: IntelliJ IDEA offers a comprehensive suite of refactoring tools that make it easy to restructure code safely and efficiently. These tools include renaming variables, extracting methods, and changing method signatures.
- **Built-in Tools and Integrations**: IntelliJ IDEA comes with built-in support for version control systems like Git, GitHub, and SVN. It also includes tools for database management, build automation (Maven, Gradle), and continuous integration.

- **User Interface**: The IDE's user interface is designed to be intuitive and customizable. It offers a range of themes and the ability to adjust fonts and colors to reduce eye strain.
- **Plugin Ecosystem**: IntelliJ IDEA has a rich ecosystem of plugins that extend its functionality. From language support to additional tools, plugins help tailor the IDE to meet specific development needs.

Editions (Community vs. Ultimate)

IntelliJ IDEA is available in two editions: Community and Ultimate. Each edition caters to different types of users and development requirements.

Community Edition

The Community Edition of IntelliJ IDEA is free and open-source, making it an excellent choice for students, hobbyists, and developers working on open-source projects. It provides essential features for Java, Kotlin, Groovy, and Scala development. Here are some key aspects of the Community Edition:

- **Java and Kotlin Support**: Full support for Java SE and Kotlin, including code completion, refactoring, and debugging.
- **Basic Refactoring Tools**: Essential refactoring tools such as renaming, moving, and extracting methods are available.
- **Version Control Systems**: Integration with Git, GitHub, and other version control systems.
- **Basic Web Development**: Limited support for HTML, CSS, and JavaScript, suitable for simple web development tasks.
- **Open-Source**: As an open-source project, the Community Edition allows for community contributions and modifications.

Ultimate Edition

The Ultimate Edition of IntelliJ IDEA is a commercial product that offers an extensive set of features designed for professional development. It supports a wide range of programming languages and technologies, making it suitable for enterprise-level projects. Here are some highlights of the Ultimate Edition:

- **Extended Language Support**: In addition to the languages supported by the Community Edition, the Ultimate Edition includes support for JavaScript, TypeScript, SQL, PHP, Ruby, Python, and more.
- **Advanced Web Development**: Comprehensive tools for modern web development, including support for frameworks like Angular, React, and Vue.js.
- **Database Tools**: Advanced database tools for managing and querying databases directly within the IDE.
- **Enterprise Features**: Support for enterprise frameworks such as Spring, Java EE, and Hibernate.
- **Integrated Tools**: Built-in tools for Docker, Kubernetes, and cloud services.
- **Performance and Analysis Tools**: Advanced profiling and performance analysis tools to optimize applications.
- **Priority Support**: Access to priority technical support from JetBrains.

Comparison with Other IDEs

IntelliJ IDEA is often compared with other popular IDEs such as Eclipse, Visual Studio Code, and NetBeans. Each IDE has its strengths and weaknesses, making them suitable for different development needs and preferences.

IntelliJ IDEA vs. Eclipse

Eclipse is another well-known IDE, particularly popular among Java developers. Here's a comparison between IntelliJ IDEA and Eclipse:

- **User Interface**: IntelliJ IDEA is praised for its modern and intuitive user interface, while Eclipse is often considered less user-friendly due to its complex and sometimes cluttered interface.
- **Performance**: IntelliJ IDEA generally offers better performance, with faster indexing and code analysis, compared to Eclipse, which can be slower, especially with large projects.
- **Features and Plugins**: Both IDEs have a rich set of features and a vast plugin ecosystem. However, IntelliJ IDEA's plugins are often considered more stable and better integrated.

- **Learning Curve**: IntelliJ IDEA has a steeper learning curve initially due to its vast array of features, but many developers find it more efficient in the long run. Eclipse, with its simpler initial setup, might be easier for beginners.
- **Community and Support**: Eclipse has a larger open-source community, while IntelliJ IDEA, particularly the Ultimate Edition, benefits from JetBrains' professional support.

IntelliJ IDEA vs. Visual Studio Code

Visual Studio Code (VS Code) is a lightweight, open-source code editor from Microsoft. It has gained immense popularity due to its flexibility and extensive extension marketplace. Here's how it compares with IntelliJ IDEA:

- **Performance**: VS Code is lightweight and fast, making it ideal for smaller projects and quick edits. IntelliJ IDEA, being a full-fledged IDE, can be heavier but offers more comprehensive tools for complex development.
- **Language Support**: VS Code supports a wide range of languages through extensions. IntelliJ IDEA, particularly the Ultimate Edition, offers native support for many languages and technologies out-of-the-box.
- **Features**: IntelliJ IDEA provides more advanced features such as refactoring, code analysis, and built-in tools for databases and version control. VS Code, while highly customizable, relies on extensions to match this functionality.
- **User Interface**: Both tools have a modern and customizable interface. However, IntelliJ IDEA offers a more integrated experience with its features, while VS Code's interface revolves around its extensions.
- **Debugging and Testing**: IntelliJ IDEA provides robust debugging and testing tools integrated into the IDE. VS Code also offers excellent debugging capabilities, but these often require additional configuration and extensions.

IntelliJ IDEA vs. NetBeans

NetBeans is another IDE commonly used for Java development. It's known for its simplicity and ease of use. Here's a comparison with IntelliJ IDEA:

- **User Interface**: IntelliJ IDEA has a more polished and modern interface compared to NetBeans, which can feel outdated.

- **Features**: IntelliJ IDEA offers more advanced features and tools for code analysis, refactoring, and integrated development compared to NetBeans.
- **Performance**: IntelliJ IDEA generally performs better with large projects due to its efficient indexing and code analysis capabilities.
- **Community and Support**: NetBeans has a strong open-source community, but IntelliJ IDEA benefits from JetBrains' continuous professional support and development.
- **Plugin Ecosystem**: While NetBeans has a good range of plugins, IntelliJ IDEA's plugin ecosystem is more extensive and better integrated.

1.2 Installing IntelliJ IDEA

Installing IntelliJ IDEA is a straightforward process that involves downloading the appropriate installer for your operating system and following the installation instructions. This section will guide you through the system requirements, downloading, and installation steps for Windows, macOS, and Linux.

System Requirements

Before installing IntelliJ IDEA, it's important to ensure that your system meets the minimum requirements to run the IDE smoothly. The following are the general system requirements for IntelliJ IDEA:

Hardware Requirements

- **Processor**: Minimum 2 GHz CPU (multi-core processor recommended)
- **Memory**: Minimum 2 GB RAM (8 GB RAM or more recommended for larger projects and better performance)
- **Storage**: Minimum 2.5 GB of free disk space, SSD recommended
- **Screen Resolution**: 1024x768 minimum screen resolution

Software Requirements

- **Operating Systems**:
  - Windows 8.1 or later
  - macOS 10.13 or later
  - Any modern Linux distribution (with GTK+ 2.18 or later and glibc 2.17 or later)

- **Java Development Kit (JDK)**: IntelliJ IDEA comes bundled with a JetBrains Runtime (a fork of OpenJDK), but you can configure it to use any compatible JDK version.

Downloading IntelliJ IDEA

To download IntelliJ IDEA, follow these steps:

1. **Visit the Official Website**: Open your web browser and go to the official JetBrains IntelliJ IDEA download page: JetBrains IntelliJ IDEA
2. **Choose the Edition**: Select either the Community Edition (free) or the Ultimate Edition (commercial). The Community Edition is suitable for most Java, Kotlin, and basic development tasks, while the Ultimate Edition offers additional features for web, enterprise, and mobile development.
3. **Select the Operating System**: Choose your operating system (Windows, macOS, or Linux) to download the appropriate installer.

Installation Steps

Windows

1. **Run the Installer**: Once the download is complete, locate the installer file (e.g., ideaIC-2023.1.exe for the Community Edition) and double-click to run it.
2. **Start Installation**: The installation wizard will open. Click "Next" to begin the installation process.
3. **Choose Installation Directory**: Select the directory where you want to install IntelliJ IDEA. The default location is usually fine, but you can choose a different location if needed. Click "Next".
4. **Select Installation Options**:
   - Create Desktop Shortcut: Optionally create a desktop shortcut for easy access.
   - Add "Open Folder as Project": Adds an option in the context menu of Windows Explorer to open a folder as a project in IntelliJ IDEA.
   - Update PATH Variable: Adds the bin directory of IntelliJ IDEA to the system PATH for easy command-line access.
   - Choose the appropriate options and click "Next".
5. **Choose Start Menu Folder**: Select the Start Menu folder where you want IntelliJ IDEA shortcuts to be created. Click "Install" to begin the installation.

6. **Complete Installation**: Once the installation is complete, you can choose to run IntelliJ IDEA immediately. Click "Finish" to exit the installer.

macOS

1. **Open the Disk Image**: Locate the downloaded .dmg file (e.g., ideaIC-2023.1.dmg for the Community Edition) and double-click to open it.
2. **Drag to Applications Folder**: In the window that appears, drag the IntelliJ IDEA icon to the Applications folder. This will copy IntelliJ IDEA to your Applications directory.
3. **Run IntelliJ IDEA**: Open the Applications folder and double-click the IntelliJ IDEA icon to launch the IDE.
4. **Initial Configuration**: The first time you run IntelliJ IDEA, you may be prompted to import settings from a previous version. If this is your first installation, choose "Do not import settings" and click "OK".
5. **Complete Installation**: Follow the on-screen instructions to complete the setup process.

Linux

1. **Extract the Tarball**: Locate the downloaded tarball file (e.g., ideaIC-2023.1.tar.gz for the Community Edition). Open a terminal and navigate to the directory where the tarball is located. Extract the contents using the following command:

   tar -xzf ideaIC-2023.1.tar.gz

2. **Move to Installation Directory**: Move the extracted directory to an appropriate location, such as /opt:

   sudo mv idea-IC-2023.1 /opt/

3. **Create a Symlink**: Create a symbolic link to make it easier to launch IntelliJ IDEA from the terminal:

   sudo ln -s /opt/idea-IC-2023.1/bin/idea.sh /usr/local/bin/idea

4. **Run IntelliJ IDEA**: Launch IntelliJ IDEA using the command:

idea

5. **Initial Configuration**: On the first run, you may be prompted to import settings from a previous version. If this is your first installation, choose "Do not import settings" and click "OK".
6. **Complete Installation**: Follow the on-screen instructions to complete the setup process.

Post-Installation Setup

Once IntelliJ IDEA is installed, there are a few additional steps you can take to optimize your development environment:

1. **Configure JDK**: If IntelliJ IDEA doesn't automatically detect your JDK, you'll need to configure it. Go to File > Project Structure > SDKs, click the + button, and select the path to your JDK installation.
2. **Install Plugins**: IntelliJ IDEA has a rich plugin ecosystem. Go to File > Settings > Plugins (or IntelliJ IDEA > Preferences > Plugins on macOS) to browse and install plugins for additional language support, frameworks, and tools.
3. **Customize the UI**: Customize the appearance of IntelliJ IDEA to suit your preferences. Go to File > Settings > Appearance & Behavior > Appearance to change the theme, font size, and other UI elements.
4. **Set Up Version Control**: Configure your version control systems (Git, GitHub, etc.) by going to File > Settings > Version Control. Add repositories and set up your version control preferences.
5. **Create a New Project**: To create a new project, go to File > New > Project, select the project type, and follow the prompts to set up your new project.

1.3 Getting Started with the IDE

Once you have installed IntelliJ IDEA, it's time to get started with the IDE. This chapter will guide you through the first launch, the initial setup wizard, and configuring JDK and SDKs, ensuring you have a solid foundation to start developing efficiently.

First Launch

Launching IntelliJ IDEA for the first time is an exciting step. The IDE will initialize its components and guide you through several configuration steps to tailor the environment to your needs.

Opening IntelliJ IDEA

1. **Windows**: Double-click the IntelliJ IDEA shortcut on your desktop or find it in the Start Menu and click to open.
2. **macOS**: Open the Applications folder and double-click the IntelliJ IDEA icon.
3. **Linux**: Open a terminal and type idea if you created a symlink; otherwise, navigate to the bin directory and run ./idea.sh.

Upon the first launch, IntelliJ IDEA will ask if you want to import settings from a previous installation. If this is your first time using IntelliJ IDEA, select "Do not import settings" and click "OK".

Initial Setup Wizard

The initial setup wizard helps configure IntelliJ IDEA according to your preferences. Follow these steps to complete the setup:

1. Choose UI Theme

IntelliJ IDEA offers two main themes:

- **Light**: A bright theme suitable for well-lit environments.
- **Dark**: A dark theme that's easier on the eyes in low-light conditions and preferred by many developers.

Select your preferred theme and click "Next".

2. Install Plugins

IntelliJ IDEA supports a wide range of plugins to enhance functionality. The setup wizard suggests popular plugins based on your development needs. You can also browse and install additional plugins later.

- **Select Recommended Plugins**: Check the boxes next to recommended plugins you want to install.
- **Browse Repositories**: Click "Browse Repositories" to explore more plugins and install any that might be useful for your work.

Once you've selected your plugins, click "Next".

3. Configure Version Control

If you plan to use version control systems like Git, configure them during the initial setup. IntelliJ IDEA can detect installed VCS software and configure it automatically.

- **Git**: If Git is installed on your system, IntelliJ IDEA will prompt you to configure it. If not, you can install Git and then configure it.
- **Other VCS**: You can configure other version control systems such as Mercurial, Subversion, and more from the settings later.

After configuring version control, click "Next".

4. Data Sharing

JetBrains collects anonymous data to improve IntelliJ IDEA. You can choose to opt-in or opt-out of this data sharing. Select your preference and click "Next".

5. Complete Setup

The setup wizard is now complete. Click "Start using IntelliJ IDEA" to finish the setup and open the IDE.

Configuring JDK and SDKs

IntelliJ IDEA requires a Java Development Kit (JDK) to run and compile Java applications. If you are developing in other languages, you might need to configure additional SDKs (Software Development Kits). Here's how to configure the JDK and other SDKs.

Configuring JDK

1. **Open Project Structure**: Go to File > Project Structure or press Ctrl+Alt+Shift+S (Cmd+; on macOS).

2. **Add JDK**:
   - o In the Project Structure dialog, select Platform Settings > SDKs.
   - o Click the + icon to add a new SDK.
   - o Select JDK from the dropdown menu.
   - o Navigate to the directory where the JDK is installed (e.g., C:\Program Files\Java\jdk-11 on Windows, /Library/Java/JavaVirtualMachines/jdk-11.jdk/Contents/Home on macOS, or /usr/lib/jvm/java-11-openjdk on Linux).
3. **Verify JDK Configuration**: IntelliJ IDEA will automatically detect the JDK version and display its details. Ensure the JDK is correctly configured and click "Apply" and then "OK".

Setting the Project SDK

Once the JDK is configured, you need to set it as the Project SDK:

1. **Project Settings**:
   - o In the Project Structure dialog, select Project Settings > Project.
   - o Under Project SDK, select the JDK you configured from the dropdown menu.
2. **Project Language Level**:
   - o Set the Project language level to match the JDK version you are using. For example, if you are using JDK 11, select "11 - Local variable syntax for lambda parameters" from the dropdown.
3. **Apply and OK**: Click "Apply" and then "OK" to save the settings.

Configuring Additional SDKs

If you are developing in other languages or using additional tools that require SDKs, you need to configure them as well. Here are some common SDK configurations:

Kotlin

1. **Open Plugin Settings**: Go to File > Settings > Plugins (or IntelliJ IDEA > Preferences > Plugins on macOS).
2. **Install Kotlin Plugin**: Search for the Kotlin plugin, install it, and restart IntelliJ IDEA if prompted.
3. **Configure Kotlin SDK**:
   - o Go to File > Project Structure.
   - o Select Platform Settings > SDKs.

- Click the + icon, select Kotlin SDK, and configure the SDK as needed.

Scala

1. **Open Plugin Settings**: Go to File > Settings > Plugins (or IntelliJ IDEA > Preferences > Plugins on macOS).
2. **Install Scala Plugin**: Search for the Scala plugin, install it, and restart IntelliJ IDEA if prompted.
3. **Configure Scala SDK**:
    - Go to File > Project Structure.
    - Select Platform Settings > SDKs.
    - Click the + icon, select Scala SDK, and configure the SDK as needed.

Other Languages and Frameworks

IntelliJ IDEA supports a wide range of languages and frameworks through plugins and additional SDK configurations. Follow similar steps to install the necessary plugins and configure the SDKs for languages like Python, Ruby, PHP, JavaScript, and frameworks like Spring, Hibernate, and more.

Creating Your First Project

After completing the initial setup and configuring the JDK and SDKs, you're ready to create your first project in IntelliJ IDEA. Follow these steps to create a new project:

1. **Create New Project**:
    - Go to File > New > Project.
    - Select the project type. For example, select Java if you are creating a Java project.
2. **Configure Project SDK**:
    - Ensure the correct SDK is selected. If not, choose the appropriate SDK from the dropdown menu.
    - Click "Next".
3. **Project Template**:
    - Choose a template if available, such as a Command Line App for a basic Java application. This step is optional and can be skipped by selecting "Next".
4. **Name and Location**:
    - Enter a project name and specify the project location.
    - Click "Finish" to create the project.

IntelliJ IDEA will set up the project structure and create necessary files based on your selections. Once the project is created, you'll be greeted with the main IDE window where you can start coding.

Navigating the IntelliJ IDEA Interface

Understanding the IntelliJ IDEA interface will help you navigate and use the IDE efficiently. Here are some key components of the interface:

- **Project Tool Window**: Located on the left side, this window displays the project structure, including files and directories. You can use it to navigate and manage your project files.
- **Editor Window**: The central area where you write and edit code. IntelliJ IDEA supports multiple tabs, allowing you to work on several files simultaneously.
- **Tool Windows**: Various tool windows are available for different tasks, such as the Version Control window for managing version control systems, the Terminal for command-line access, and the Database window for managing database connections.
- **Status Bar**: Located at the bottom, the status bar provides information about the current project and IDE status, including errors, warnings, and background tasks.

1.4 Overview of the User Interface

IntelliJ IDEA is renowned for its intuitive and customizable user interface, designed to enhance developer productivity and streamline workflow. This section provides a comprehensive overview of the main window components, tool windows, editor tabs, and the navigation bar. Understanding these elements will help you navigate the IDE effectively and utilize its features to their fullest potential.

Main Window Components

The main window of IntelliJ IDEA is the central hub where you interact with your projects. It is composed of several key components, each serving a specific purpose:

1. Menu Bar

The menu bar is located at the top of the window and provides access to all the commands and settings available in IntelliJ IDEA. The menu items include:

- **File**: Create new projects, open existing projects, manage settings, and exit the IDE.
- **Edit**: Access editing commands such as cut, copy, paste, undo, redo, and find/replace.
- **View**: Toggle the visibility of tool windows and customize the appearance of the IDE.
- **Navigate**: Navigate through the project files, classes, symbols, and more.
- **Code**: Access code generation, completion, and formatting options.
- **Analyze**: Perform code inspections and view analysis reports.
- **Refactor**: Access refactoring tools for improving code structure.
- **Build**: Build and compile projects, run tests, and manage build configurations.
- **Run**: Run, debug, and profile applications.
- **Tools**: Access additional tools such as version control, terminal, database tools, and more.
- **Help**: Access IntelliJ IDEA documentation, support, and product information.

2. Toolbar

The toolbar, located just below the menu bar, provides quick access to frequently used commands and actions. It includes buttons for running and debugging applications, managing version control, and other commonly used features.

3. Project Tool Window

The Project tool window, located on the left side of the main window, displays the project structure in a tree view. It shows the files and directories that make up your project, allowing you to navigate and manage them easily. You can open files by double-clicking them or perform various file operations through the context menu.

4. Editor Window

The editor window is the central area where you write and edit your code. It supports multiple tabs, allowing you to work on several files simultaneously. The editor provides features like syntax highlighting, code completion, error detection, and inline documentation, making it easier to write and understand code.

5. Tool Windows

Tool windows provide additional functionality and are docked around the edges of the main window. They can be toggled on or off as needed. Common tool windows include:

- **Project**: Displays the project structure.
- **Version Control**: Provides version control operations and displays the status of files.
- **Terminal**: Access a built-in terminal for command-line operations.
- **Database**: Manage database connections and execute SQL queries.
- **Run/Debug**: Display the output and status of running or debugging applications.

6. Status Bar

The status bar, located at the bottom of the main window, provides information about the current project and IDE status. It displays details such as the current VCS branch, code inspection results, and background tasks. The status bar also includes widgets for quick access to various settings and tools.

Tool Windows

Tool windows in IntelliJ IDEA are designed to provide additional functionality and information, helping you manage different aspects of your development environment. They can be opened, closed, and docked around the edges of the main window. Here are some of the most commonly used tool windows:

1. Project Tool Window

The Project tool window displays the structure of your project in a hierarchical tree view. It allows you to navigate through your project's files and directories, open files for editing, and perform file operations. You can also use it to manage multiple projects within the same window.

2. Version Control Tool Window

The Version Control tool window provides a comprehensive interface for managing version control operations. It integrates with various VCS systems like Git, Mercurial, and SVN, allowing you to commit changes, view history, resolve conflicts, and manage branches. The tool window displays the status of files, highlighting changes and conflicts.

3. Terminal Tool Window

The Terminal tool window provides a built-in terminal emulator, allowing you to execute command-line operations directly within IntelliJ IDEA. It supports multiple tabs, enabling you to run several terminal sessions simultaneously. The terminal is useful for running build scripts, managing version control, and executing other command-line tasks.

4. Database Tool Window

The Database tool window allows you to manage database connections and interact with databases. You can execute SQL queries, browse database schemas, and view table data. The tool window supports various databases, including MySQL, PostgreSQL, Oracle, and more, making it a powerful tool for database management and development.

5. Run/Debug Tool Window

The Run/Debug tool window displays the output and status of running or debugging applications. It provides information about the current execution state, including variables, call stack, and console output. The tool window also includes controls for managing breakpoints, stepping through code, and terminating processes.

6. Find Tool Window

The Find tool window allows you to search for text, files, and symbols within your project. It provides powerful search capabilities, including regular expressions, case sensitivity, and scope filtering. The tool window displays search results in a list, allowing you to navigate to occurrences and perform actions on them.

7. Structure Tool Window

The Structure tool window displays the structure of the currently open file, showing elements such as classes, methods, fields, and functions. It provides a quick way to navigate within the file and understand its organization. The tool window also allows you to perform operations on the elements, such as renaming or finding usages.

Editor Tabs and Navigation Bar

The editor in IntelliJ IDEA supports multiple tabs, allowing you to work on several files simultaneously. The navigation bar provides quick access to the current file and its location within the project structure.

Editor Tabs

Editor tabs are displayed at the top of the editor window and represent the open files. Each tab shows the file name and can be customized with icons and colors to indicate the file type or status. Here are some useful features of editor tabs:

- **Switching Tabs**: Click on a tab to switch to the corresponding file. You can also use keyboard shortcuts (Ctrl+Tab on Windows/Linux, Cmd+ on macOS) to cycle through open tabs.
- **Closing Tabs**: Click the close button on a tab or use the shortcut (Ctrl+F4 on Windows/Linux, Cmd+W on macOS) to close the current tab.
- **Splitting Tabs**: Right-click a tab and select Split Vertically or Split Horizontally to view multiple files side by side. This is useful for comparing files or working on related code.
- **Pinning Tabs**: Right-click a tab and select Pin Tab to keep it open, preventing it from being closed automatically when opening new files.

Navigation Bar

The navigation bar, located at the top of the editor window, provides quick access to the current file and its location within the project structure. It displays the path to the file, including directories and packages. Here are some useful features of the navigation bar:

- **Breadcrumb Navigation**: Click on any element in the path to navigate to that directory or package. This allows you to quickly jump to different parts of your project.
- **Context Menu**: Right-click an element in the path to open a context menu with actions such as Open, Show in Explorer, Copy Path, and more.

- **File Operations**: Use the navigation bar to perform file operations such as renaming, moving, and deleting files. These actions are available through the context menu.

1.5 Customizing Your Workspace

Customizing your workspace in IntelliJ IDEA can significantly enhance your productivity and make the development process more enjoyable. IntelliJ IDEA offers a wide range of customization options, from changing the overall theme and appearance to configuring specific layouts and setting up preferences. This chapter will guide you through these customization options, helping you tailor the IDE to your needs.

Themes and Appearance

IntelliJ IDEA provides several themes and appearance settings that you can adjust to make the IDE visually appealing and comfortable to use for long periods. Here are the steps to customize themes and appearance:

Changing Themes

1. **Access Appearance Settings**:
   - Go to File > Settings (or IntelliJ IDEA > Preferences on macOS).
   - Navigate to Appearance & Behavior > Appearance.
2. **Select a Theme**:
   - In the Theme dropdown, you can choose between the default themes: IntelliJ Light, Darcula, and High Contrast.
   - IntelliJ Light provides a bright, clean interface.
   - Darcula offers a dark theme, which is easier on the eyes, especially in low-light environments.
   - High Contrast is designed for users with visual impairments.
3. **Apply and Save**:
   - After selecting a theme, click Apply and then OK to apply the changes.

Customizing Fonts and Colors

1. **Access Font Settings**:

- o Go to File > Settings (or IntelliJ IDEA > Preferences on macOS).
- o Navigate to Editor > Font.

2. **Change Font Family and Size**:
   - o Select the desired font family from the Font dropdown.
   - o Adjust the font size to your preference. A larger font size can reduce eye strain during extended coding sessions.

3. **Color Scheme**:
   - o Navigate to Editor > Color Scheme.
   - o You can select from predefined color schemes or create a custom scheme by modifying individual color settings for syntax highlighting, background, and more.

4. **Apply and Save**:
   - o Click Apply and then OK to save your changes.

Configuring Layouts

The layout of IntelliJ IDEA can be customized to fit your workflow. You can rearrange tool windows, split the editor, and configure different views to optimize your workspace.

Tool Window Layout

1. **Docking Tool Windows**:
   - o Tool windows can be docked to the sides of the main window. To dock a tool window, click and drag its title bar to the desired location.
   - o You can also use the View > Tool Windows menu to toggle the visibility of specific tool windows.

2. **Floating and Splitting Tool Windows**:
   - o Right-click the title bar of a tool window and select Floating Mode to make it a floating window.
   - o You can split tool windows to view multiple tool windows simultaneously. Right-click the title bar and select Split Mode.

3. **Resizing Tool Windows**:
   - o Drag the edges of a tool window to resize it. This allows you to allocate more space to the editor or specific tool windows as needed.

Editor Layout

1. **Splitting the Editor**:
   - To view multiple files side by side, you can split the editor window. Right-click on an editor tab and select Split Vertically or Split Horizontally.
   - You can create multiple splits and drag files between them for easy comparison and multi-file editing.
2. **Navigating Between Splits**:
   - Use Ctrl+Tab (Windows/Linux) or Cmd+Tab (macOS) to switch between open files and editor splits quickly.
   - You can also click on the tabs or use the navigation bar to move between splits.
3. **Full-Screen Mode**:
   - IntelliJ IDEA supports full-screen mode to maximize the editing space. Press Shift+F11 to toggle full-screen mode on and off.

Setting Up Preferences and Settings

IntelliJ IDEA allows extensive customization of preferences and settings to match your development style and requirements. Here are some key areas you might want to configure:

General Settings

1. **Access General Settings**:
   - Go to File > Settings (or IntelliJ IDEA > Preferences on macOS).
2. **Appearance & Behavior**:
   - In Appearance & Behavior > System Settings, you can configure various options such as the IDE theme, window settings, and keymap.
3. **Keymap**:
   - Navigate to Keymap to customize keyboard shortcuts. You can create your own keymap profile or modify an existing one to assign shortcuts that enhance your productivity.

Editor Settings

1. **Code Style**:

- Go to Editor > Code Style to configure the formatting rules for different programming languages. You can adjust indentation, brace placement, and other formatting options.
- Apply consistent code style settings across your team by exporting and importing code style schemes.

2. **General Editor Settings**:
    - In Editor > General, you can configure various aspects of the editor, such as caret behavior, code completion, and scroll settings.
    - Enable or disable features like soft wraps, line numbers, and method separators.

3. **Live Templates**:
    - Navigate to Editor > Live Templates to create and manage code snippets. Live templates allow you to insert frequently used code patterns quickly.
    - Define your own templates or modify existing ones to suit your coding style.

Version Control Settings

1. **Configure Version Control Systems**:
    - Go to Version Control > Git (or other VCS) to configure settings for your version control system. You can set up repositories, manage credentials, and configure push/pull settings.
    - Customize commit message templates and hooks to enforce consistent commit practices.

2. **File Status Highlighting**:
    - In Version Control > File Status Highlighting, configure how file statuses are displayed in the editor and project view. This helps you quickly identify modified, added, or deleted files.

Build, Execution, Deployment Settings

1. **Compiler Settings**:
    - Go to Build, Execution, Deployment > Compiler to configure compiler settings. You can specify the compiler to use, configure annotation processors, and set up build output directories.

2. **Run/Debug Configurations**:

- o Navigate to Build, Execution, Deployment > Run/Debug Configurations to create and manage configurations for running and debugging applications. Define configurations for different environments, command-line arguments, and JVM options.
3. **Deployment Settings**:
   - o In Build, Execution, Deployment > Deployment, configure settings for deploying applications to various environments. Set up remote servers, configure deployment paths, and manage deployment configurations.

Plugin Management

1. **Installing Plugins**:
   - o Go to File > Settings > Plugins (or IntelliJ IDEA > Preferences > Plugins on macOS) to browse and install plugins. IntelliJ IDEA's plugin repository offers a wide range of plugins for different languages, frameworks, and tools.
2. **Managing Installed Plugins**:
   - o In the Plugins settings, you can enable, disable, update, or uninstall plugins. Keep your plugins up to date to benefit from the latest features and improvements.

Conclusion

Customizing your workspace in IntelliJ IDEA involves adjusting themes and appearance, configuring layouts, and setting up preferences and settings. These customizations help create a comfortable and efficient development environment tailored to your specific needs and preferences. By leveraging the extensive customization options available in IntelliJ IDEA, you can enhance your productivity, reduce eye strain, and streamline your workflow. Whether you're working on a small project or managing a large codebase, a well-configured workspace can make a significant difference in your overall development experience.

Chapter 2: Creating and Managing Projects

2.1 Creating a New Project

Creating and managing projects in IntelliJ IDEA is foundational to leveraging its powerful capabilities. This chapter will guide you through the process of creating a new project, exploring various project types and templates, setting up the Project SDK, and walking through the Project Wizard. By the end of this chapter, you will be equipped with the knowledge to create and configure projects efficiently, laying a strong foundation for productive development.

Project Types and Templates

IntelliJ IDEA supports a wide range of project types and templates to cater to different development needs. Understanding these options will help you choose the most suitable template for your specific project requirements.

Project Types

1. **Java Projects**:
   - **Standard Java Projects**: Suitable for standalone Java applications and libraries.
   - **Java Enterprise (JEE) Projects**: Ideal for enterprise-level applications, supporting frameworks like Spring, Hibernate, and Java EE technologies.
2. **Kotlin Projects**:
   - **Standard Kotlin Projects**: For Kotlin applications and libraries.
   - **Kotlin/JVM**: For Kotlin projects targeting the Java Virtual Machine (JVM).
3. **Python Projects**:
   - **Standard Python Projects**: For developing Python applications, scripts, and libraries.
   - **Django Projects**: For web development using the Django framework.
4. **Web Projects**:
   - **JavaScript/TypeScript Projects**: For front-end development using JavaScript or TypeScript.
   - **Node.js Projects**: For server-side development using Node.js.

- o **Angular/React/Vue.js Projects**: For developing single-page applications using popular front-end frameworks.
5. **Mobile Projects**:
    - o **Android Projects**: For developing Android applications using the Android SDK.
    - o **Flutter Projects**: For cross-platform mobile applications using the Flutter framework.
6. **Data Science Projects**:
    - o **R Projects**: For data analysis and statistical computing using the R programming language.
    - o **Jupyter Notebooks**: For interactive data science and machine learning projects.

Project Templates

IntelliJ IDEA offers various templates to kickstart your projects with predefined settings and configurations. These templates can save time and provide a structured starting point for different types of projects.

1. **Command Line Application**:
    - o A basic template for creating command-line applications with boilerplate code for input/output handling.
2. **JavaFX Application**:
    - o A template for developing desktop applications using JavaFX, including sample code for UI components.
3. **Spring Boot Application**:
    - o A template for creating Spring Boot applications with integrated dependencies and configuration for rapid development.
4. **Maven/Gradle Project**:
    - o Templates for creating projects with build automation tools like Maven and Gradle, including sample build scripts.
5. **Web Application**:
    - o A template for developing web applications with sample configurations for servlets, JSP, and web.xml.
6. **Microservices Project**:
    - o A template for building microservices architectures using frameworks like Spring Cloud and Docker.

Setting Up Project SDK

The Software Development Kit (SDK) is crucial for any project in IntelliJ IDEA. It provides the necessary libraries and tools for developing applications. Setting up the correct SDK ensures that your project compiles and runs successfully.

Installing an SDK

1. **Java SDK**:
   - Download the latest Java Development Kit (JDK) from the official Oracle website or OpenJDK.
   - Install the JDK on your system by following the installation instructions specific to your operating system.
2. **Kotlin SDK**:
   - Kotlin projects typically use the JDK, but you can also download the Kotlin compiler from the official Kotlin website.
3. **Python SDK**:
   - Download and install Python from the official Python website.
4. **Android SDK**:
   - Install Android Studio, which includes the Android SDK, from the Android Studio website.
5. **Other SDKs**:
   - For other languages and frameworks, refer to the respective official websites for installation instructions.

Configuring Project SDK

1. **Open Project Structure**:
   - Go to File > Project Structure (or use the shortcut Ctrl+Alt+Shift+S on Windows/Linux, Cmd+; on macOS).
2. **Add SDK**:
   - In the Project Structure dialog, navigate to Platform Settings > SDKs.
   - Click the + button to add a new SDK.
   - Select the appropriate SDK type (e.g., JDK, Python SDK, Android SDK).
3. **Specify SDK Path**:
   - Browse to the installation path of the SDK and select it.
   - IntelliJ IDEA will automatically detect the SDK and configure it.
4. **Set Project SDK**:
   - In the Project Settings > Project section, select the configured SDK from the Project SDK dropdown.

o   Apply the changes and click OK.

Project Wizard Walkthrough

IntelliJ IDEA's Project Wizard simplifies the process of creating a new project. It guides you through the necessary steps, ensuring your project is set up correctly with all required dependencies.

Step-by-Step Walkthrough

1. **Launch IntelliJ IDEA**:
    o   Open IntelliJ IDEA. If it's already running, go to File > New > Project.
2. **Select Project Type**:
    o   The New Project dialog will appear.
    o   Select the desired project type from the left-hand list (e.g., Java, Kotlin, Python, JavaScript, Android).
3. **Choose Project SDK**:
    o   If the SDK is already configured, select it from the Project SDK dropdown.
    o   If not, click New... to configure a new SDK as described in the previous section.
4. **Select Project Template**:
    o   Depending on the selected project type, you will see various templates. Choose the appropriate template for your project.
    o   For example, if you selected Java, you might choose JavaFX Application or Command Line Application.
5. **Configure Project Name and Location**:
    o   Enter the Project Name.
    o   Specify the Project Location where the project files will be stored.
    o   Click Next.
6. **Customize Project Settings**:
    o   Depending on the selected template, you may need to configure additional settings such as group ID, artifact ID, and version for Maven/Gradle projects.
    o   Click Next or Finish once all settings are configured.
7. **Review Project Structure**:
    o   IntelliJ IDEA will generate the project based on your settings.
    o   Review the project structure in the Project tool window to ensure everything is set up correctly.
8. **Start Coding**:

- o Open the generated source files in the editor and start coding.
- o You can run or debug the project using the toolbar buttons or corresponding shortcuts.

Practical Example: Creating a Java Project

Let's walk through creating a standard Java project using IntelliJ IDEA.

1. **Launch IntelliJ IDEA** and select Create New Project.
2. **Select Project Type**:
   - o Choose Java from the list on the left.
   - o Ensure you have the JDK installed and select it from the Project SDK dropdown.
3. **Choose Project Template**:
   - o Select Command Line Application.
4. **Configure Project Name and Location**:
   - o Enter MyFirstJavaProject as the project name.
   - o Specify the location, e.g., C:\Projects\MyFirstJavaProject.
   - o Click Next.
5. **Customize Project Settings**:
   - o Since this is a simple command-line application, no additional settings are needed.
   - o Click Finish.
6. **Review Project Structure**:
   - o IntelliJ IDEA creates a basic project structure with a src folder for source files.
   - o The Main class with a main method is generated automatically.
7. **Start Coding**:
   - o Open the Main.java file in the editor.
   - o You should see the following boilerplate code:

```java
public class Main {
    public static void main(String[] args) {
System.out.println("Hello, World!");
    }
}
```

8. **Run the Project**:
   - o Click the Run button in the toolbar or use the shortcut Shift+F10.
   - o The output should display Hello, World! in the Run tool window.

Practical Example: Creating a Python Project

Next, let's create a Python project using IntelliJ IDEA.

1. **Launch IntelliJ IDEA** and select Create New Project.
2. **Select Project Type**:
    o Choose Python from the list on the left.
    o Ensure you have Python installed and select it from the Project SDK dropdown.
3. **Choose Project Template**:
    o Select Pure Python.
4. **Configure Project Name and Location**:
    o Enter MyFirstPythonProject as the project name.
    o Specify the location, e.g., C:\Projects\MyFirstPythonProject.
    o Click Create.
5. **Review Project Structure**:
    o IntelliJ IDEA creates a basic project structure with a main.py file.
6. **Start Coding**:
    o Open the main.py file in the editor.
    o You should see the following boilerplate code:

```
if __name__ == '__main__':
print("Hello, World!")
```

7. **Run the Project**:
    o Click the Run button in the toolbar or use the shortcut Shift+F10.
    o The output should display Hello, World! in the Run tool window.

Practical Example: Creating a Web Project with React

Finally, let's create a web project using the React framework.

1. **Launch IntelliJ IDEA** and select Create New Project.
2. **Select Project Type**:
    o Choose JavaScript from the list on the left.
    o Ensure you have Node.js installed and select it from the Node.js Interpreter dropdown.
3. **Choose Project Template**:
    o Select React App.

4. **Configure Project Name and Location**:
    - o Enter MyFirstReactApp as the project name.
    - o Specify the location, e.g., C:\Projects\MyFirstReactApp.
    - o Click Next.
5. **Customize Project Settings**:
    - o No additional settings are needed for a basic React app.
    - o Click Finish.
6. **Review Project Structure**:
    - o IntelliJ IDEA creates a project structure typical for React applications, with folders like public and src.
7. **Start Coding**:
    - o Open the App.js file in the src folder.
    - o You should see the following boilerplate code:

```
importReactfrom'react';
import logo from'./logo.svg';
import'./App.css';

functionApp() {
return (
<divclassName="App">
<headerclassName="App-header">
<imgsrc={logo}className="App-logo"alt="logo" />
<p>
     Edit <code>src/App.js</code> and save to reload.
</p>
<a
className="App-link"
href="https://reactjs.org"
target="_blank"
rel="noopenernoreferrer"
>
     Learn React
</a>
</header>
</div>
  );
}
```

exportdefaultApp;

8. **Run the Project**:
   - Open the terminal in IntelliJ IDEA and run npm start.
   - The development server will start, and you can view your React app in the browser at http://localhost:3000.

2.2 Importing Existing Projects

Importing existing projects into IntelliJ IDEA is a common task for developers who need to work on legacy codebases, collaborate with team members, or switch between different development environments. IntelliJ IDEA offers robust support for importing projects from various sources, including version control systems and external build tools like Maven and Gradle. This chapter will guide you through the process of importing existing projects, handling potential import conflicts, and ensuring a smooth transition into the IntelliJ IDEA environment.

Importing from Version Control

IntelliJ IDEA integrates seamlessly with various version control systems (VCS), such as Git, Mercurial, and Subversion. This integration allows you to clone repositories directly into the IDE and manage your code versioning effortlessly.

Cloning a Repository

1. **Access the VCS Menu**:
   - Open IntelliJ IDEA.
   - Navigate to VCS > Get from Version Control.
2. **Select VCS Type**:
   - In the Get from Version Control dialog, choose the version control system you are using (e.g., Git).
3. **Enter Repository URL**:
   - Enter the URL of the repository you want to clone.
   - Specify the Parent Directory where the project should be cloned.

- o Enter the Directory Name for the cloned project.

4. **Authenticate (if necessary)**:
   - o If the repository requires authentication, provide your credentials.
   - o IntelliJ IDEA supports SSH keys and personal access tokens for secure authentication.

5. **Clone the Repository**:
   - o Click Clone to start the cloning process.
   - o IntelliJ IDEA will download the repository and set up the project in the specified directory.

6. **Open the Project**:
   - o Once the cloning is complete, IntelliJ IDEA will prompt you to open the newly cloned project.
   - o Click Yes to open the project in a new window or the current window.

Importing an Existing Local Repository

1. **Open the Project from Disk**:
   - o If you have a local repository already cloned on your disk, go to File > New > Project from Existing Sources.

2. **Select the Project Directory**:
   - o Browse to the directory containing your local repository and select it.
   - o Click OK.

3. **Choose Import Method**:
   - o IntelliJ IDEA will prompt you to select how you want to open the project. Choose Open as Project.

4. **Configure VCS Root**:
   - o IntelliJ IDEA will automatically detect the version control system used by the project.
   - o If the VCS root is not detected automatically, go to File > Settings (or IntelliJ IDEA > Preferences on macOS), navigate to Version Control, and add the project root manually.

5. **Complete the Import**:
   - o Click Finish to complete the import process.
   - o IntelliJ IDEA will index the project files and set up the version control integration.

Importing from External Models (Maven, Gradle)

IntelliJ IDEA provides excellent support for external build tools like Maven and Gradle. These tools define project structure, dependencies, and build configurations, making it easy to manage and import projects.

Importing a Maven Project

1. **Open the Project from Disk**:
   o Go to File > New > Project from Existing Sources.
2. **Select the Project Directory**:
   o Browse to the directory containing your Maven project (typically the directory with the pom.xml file) and select it.
   o Click OK.
3. **Choose Import Method**:
   o IntelliJ IDEA will detect the presence of a pom.xml file and prompt you to import the project as a Maven project.
   o Choose Import project from external model and select Maven.
4. **Import Project Settings**:
   o In the Import Project from Maven dialog, configure the following settings:
      ▪ **Import Maven projects automatically**: Check this option to enable automatic import and synchronization of the Maven project.
      ▪ **VM options for importer**: Specify any JVM options if needed for the import process.
      ▪ **Profiles**: Select the Maven profiles you want to activate during the import.
5. **Complete the Import**:
   o Click Next and review the detected project structure and dependencies.
   o Click Finish to complete the import process.
   o IntelliJ IDEA will resolve dependencies, download necessary libraries, and set up the project according to the Maven configuration.

Importing a Gradle Project

1. **Open the Project from Disk**:
   o Go to File > New > Project from Existing Sources.

2. **Select the Project Directory**:
   - ○ Browse to the directory containing your Gradle project (typically the directory with the build.gradle file) and select it.
   - ○ Click OK.
3. **Choose Import Method**:
   - ○ IntelliJ IDEA will detect the presence of a build.gradle file and prompt you to import the project as a Gradle project.
   - ○ Choose Import project from external model and select Gradle.
4. **Import Project Settings**:
   - ○ In the Import Project from Gradle dialog, configure the following settings:
     - ▪ **Use auto-import**: Check this option to enable automatic import and synchronization of the Gradle project.
     - ▪ **Create separate module per source set**: Check this option to create separate modules for each source set in the project.
     - ▪ **Gradle JVM**: Specify the JVM to use for running Gradle.
5. **Complete the Import**:
   - ○ Click Next and review the detected project structure and dependencies.
   - ○ Click Finish to complete the import process.
   - ○ IntelliJ IDEA will resolve dependencies, download necessary libraries, and set up the project according to the Gradle configuration.

Handling Import Conflicts

Importing projects can sometimes lead to conflicts, especially when dealing with complex projects or different environments. IntelliJ IDEA provides tools and options to handle these conflicts effectively.

Common Import Conflicts

1. **Dependency Conflicts**:
   - ○ Conflicts can occur when different versions of the same dependency are specified in the project configuration.
   - ○ IntelliJ IDEA may display warnings or errors related to dependency resolution.
2. **Module Naming Conflicts**:

- o When importing multiple modules, naming conflicts can arise if modules have the same name.
- o IntelliJ IDEA may prompt you to resolve these conflicts by renaming modules.

3. **Configuration Conflicts**:
   - o Configuration conflicts can occur if the project's settings are incompatible with the current IntelliJ IDEA configuration.
   - o This can include issues with SDK versions, compiler settings, or build tool configurations.

Resolving Dependency Conflicts

1. **View Dependency Hierarchy**:
   - o Go to View > Tool Windows > Maven/Gradle (depending on your project type).
   - o In the Maven/Gradle tool window, expand the Dependencies section to view the project's dependency hierarchy.
   - o This view helps identify conflicting dependencies and their transitive dependencies.

2. **Exclude Conflicting Dependencies**:
   - o Open the pom.xml (for Maven) or build.gradle (for Gradle) file.
   - o Add exclusions for conflicting dependencies to resolve version conflicts.
   - o Example for Maven:

     ```xml
     Copy code
     <dependency>
     <groupId>com.example</groupId>
     <artifactId>example-dependency</artifactId>
     <version>1.0.0</version>
     <exclusions>
     <exclusion>
     <groupId>com.example.conflict</groupId>
     <artifactId>conflicting-dependency</artifactId>
     </exclusion>
     </exclusions>
     </dependency>
     ```

   - o Example for Gradle:

```
gradle
Copy code
dependencies {
    implementation('com.example:example-dependency:1.0.0') {
        exclude group: 'com.example.conflict', module: 'conflicting-dependency'
    }
}
```

3. **Use Dependency Management**:
   - For Maven, use the <dependencyManagement> section in the pom.xml to specify dependency versions globally.
   - For Gradle, use the resolutionStrategy in the build.gradle to force specific versions.
   - Example for Maven:

```xml
xml
Copy code
<dependencyManagement>
<dependencies>
<dependency>
<groupId>com.example</groupId>
<artifactId>example-dependency</artifactId>
<version>1.0.0</version>
</dependency>
</dependencies>
</dependencyManagement>
```

   - Example for Gradle:

```gradle
gradle
Copy code
configurations.all {
resolutionStrategy {
    force 'com.example:example-dependency:1.0.0'
  }
}
```

Resolving Module Naming Conflicts

1. **Rename Modules**:

- o Go to File > Project Structure (or Ctrl+Alt+Shift+S on Windows/Linux, Cmd+; on macOS).
- o Navigate to Modules and select the conflicting module.
- o Click the Rename button and provide a unique name for the module.

2. **Adjust Module Configuration**:
   - o Review the module configuration to ensure it matches the project requirements.
   - o Adjust settings such as content roots, dependencies, and module SDKs as needed.

3. **Resolve Path Conflicts**:
   - o Ensure that module paths do not conflict with each other.
   - o Adjust the module content roots or exclude specific directories to prevent overlap.

Resolving Configuration Conflicts

1. **Check Project SDK**:
   - o Ensure the project SDK is correctly configured.
   - o Go to File > Project Structure > Project and verify the Project SDK setting.
   - o If necessary, add or update the SDK to match the project requirements.

2. **Adjust Compiler Settings**:
   - o Go to File > Settings > Build, Execution, Deployment > Compiler (or IntelliJ IDEA > Preferences on macOS).
   - o Review and adjust compiler settings to ensure compatibility with the project.

3. **Update Build Tool Configurations**:
   - o For Maven projects, check the settings.xml file for any custom configurations that may affect the project.
   - o For Gradle projects, review the gradle.properties and settings.gradle files for any custom settings.

4. **Reimport the Project**:
   - o If you encounter persistent issues, try reimporting the project.
   - o Go to File > Synchronize to refresh the project structure and dependencies.
   - o Alternatively, close the project and reopen it to trigger a full reimport.

Practical Example: Importing a Java Maven Project

Let's walk through importing a Java Maven project into IntelliJ IDEA.

1. **Open IntelliJ IDEA** and select File > New > Project from Existing Sources.
2. **Select the Project Directory**:
   o Browse to the directory containing the Maven project and select the pom.xml file.
   o Click OK.
3. **Choose Import Method**:
   o IntelliJ IDEA will detect the pom.xml file and prompt you to import the project as a Maven project.
   o Select Import project from external model and choose Maven.
4. **Import Project Settings**:
   o Check the Import Maven projects automatically option.
   o Click Next.
5. **Complete the Import**:
   o Review the detected project structure and dependencies.
   o Click Finish to complete the import process.
   o IntelliJ IDEA will resolve dependencies, download necessary libraries, and set up the project according to the Maven configuration.
6. **Handle Dependency Conflicts**:
   o Open the Maven tool window to review the dependency hierarchy.
   o Resolve any conflicts by excluding conflicting dependencies or using dependency management.
7. **Start Coding**:
   o Once the import process is complete and conflicts are resolved, you can start coding and running your Maven project in IntelliJ IDEA.

Practical Example: Importing a Gradle Project

Next, let's import a Gradle project into IntelliJ IDEA.

1. **Open IntelliJ IDEA** and select File > New > Project from Existing Sources.
2. **Select the Project Directory**:
   o Browse to the directory containing the Gradle project and select the build.gradle file.
   o Click OK.

3. **Choose Import Method**:
   - IntelliJ IDEA will detect the build.gradle file and prompt you to import the project as a Gradle project.
   - Select Import project from external model and choose Gradle.
4. **Import Project Settings**:
   - Check the Use auto-import option.
   - Click Next.
5. **Complete the Import**:
   - Review the detected project structure and dependencies.
   - Click Finish to complete the import process.
   - IntelliJ IDEA will resolve dependencies, download necessary libraries, and set up the project according to the Gradle configuration.
6. **Handle Dependency Conflicts**:
   - Open the Gradle tool window to review the dependency hierarchy.
   - Resolve any conflicts by excluding conflicting dependencies or using resolution strategies.
7. **Start Coding**:
   - Once the import process is complete and conflicts are resolved, you can start coding and running your Gradle project in IntelliJ IDEA.

Conclusion

Importing existing projects into IntelliJ IDEA is a straightforward process, whether you are working with version control systems or external build tools like Maven and Gradle. By following the steps outlined in this chapter, you can seamlessly import projects, resolve conflicts, and configure your development environment for maximum productivity. IntelliJ IDEA's powerful integration capabilities and robust handling of dependencies and configurations make it an ideal choice for managing complex projects and collaborating with team members.

2.3 Managing Project Structures

A well-organized project structure is crucial for maintaining clarity and efficiency in your development workflow. IntelliJ IDEA provides powerful tools to help you manage your project's structure, dependencies, and modules. This chapter will delve into the intricacies of project structures in IntelliJ IDEA, exploring the differences between projects and modules, configuring project structures, and managing dependencies effectively.

Project vs. Module

Understanding the distinction between projects and modules is fundamental to managing your project structure in IntelliJ IDEA.

Projects

A project in IntelliJ IDEA is the highest-level organizational unit. It encompasses all the source code, libraries, and resources needed to develop an application. A project typically represents a complete application or a large software system.

Key Characteristics of Projects:

1. **Global Settings**: Projects contain settings that apply to the entire codebase, such as version control configurations, code styles, and inspection profiles.
2. **Project SDK**: Each project can be associated with a specific Software Development Kit (SDK) that provides the runtime environment and compiler.
3. **Project Files**: Projects include configuration files such as .idea directory, which stores project-specific settings, and the project.iml file, which contains module-specific settings.

Modules

Modules are smaller units within a project that represent a sub-section of the codebase. Each module can have its own content roots, dependencies, and configurations. Modules can be independently developed, tested, and deployed.

Key Characteristics of Modules:

1. **Content Roots**: Modules have their own content roots, including source code, test code, and resource files.
2. **Dependencies**: Modules can depend on other modules within the same project or on external libraries.

3. **Modularity**: Modules facilitate modular development, allowing different parts of the application to be developed and maintained independently.

Example: Consider a web application project with the following structure:

- **Project: MyWebApp**
    - **Module: WebModule** (handles web-related functionalities)
    - **Module: ServiceModule** (handles business logic and services)
    - **Module: DataModule** (handles data persistence)

Configuring Project Structure

Configuring the project structure in IntelliJ IDEA involves setting up the content roots, source directories, libraries, and dependencies for each module. This setup ensures that the IDE can properly understand and manage your codebase.

Accessing Project Structure Settings

1. **Open Project Structure**:
    - Go to File > Project Structure or use the shortcut Ctrl+Alt+Shift+S (Windows/Linux) or Cmd+; (macOS).
2. **Project Settings**:
    - In the Project Structure dialog, you'll find several tabs for configuring different aspects of your project:
        - **Project**: Configure the project SDK and project language level.
        - **Modules**: Manage your project's modules, including content roots, dependencies, and module-specific settings.
        - **Libraries**: Add and manage libraries that are shared across multiple modules.

Configuring Modules

1. **Adding a New Module**:
    - In the Modules tab, click the + button to add a new module.
    - Select the module type (e.g., Java, Web, Maven, Gradle) and follow the wizard to set up the module.
2. **Configuring Content Roots**:

- Select a module and navigate to the Sources tab.
- Add content roots by clicking the + button and specifying the directory paths.
- Mark directories as Sources, Test Sources, Resources, or Test Resources.

3. **Managing Module Dependencies**:
   - Select the Dependencies tab within a module.
   - Add dependencies by clicking the + button and choosing from the following options:
     - **Module Dependency**: Add a dependency on another module within the project.
     - **Library**: Add a dependency on an external library.
     - **JARs or directories**: Add a dependency on specific JAR files or directories.

Configuring Libraries

1. **Adding Project Libraries**:
   - In the Libraries tab, click the + button to add a new library.
   - Choose the library type (e.g., Java, Kotlin, JavaScript) and specify the library files (JARs, directories).
2. **Assigning Libraries to Modules**:
   - After adding a library, assign it to specific modules by selecting the module and adding the library under the Dependencies tab.

Dependencies Management

Managing dependencies effectively is crucial for ensuring that your project builds and runs correctly. IntelliJ IDEA provides robust tools for managing both module dependencies and external library dependencies.

Managing Module Dependencies

Module dependencies define how different modules within a project rely on each other. Properly configuring these dependencies ensures that the modules can interact and share resources as needed.

1. **Adding Module Dependencies**:
   - Go to File > Project Structure > Modules.
   - Select the module that requires the dependency.
   - Navigate to the Dependencies tab.
   - Click the + button and choose Module Dependency.
   - Select the module you want to add as a dependency and click OK.
2. **Configuring Dependency Scope**:
   - After adding a module dependency, you can configure its scope:
     - **Compile**: The dependency is available at compile-time and runtime.
     - **Provided**: The dependency is provided by the runtime environment and is only needed at compile-time.
     - **Runtime**: The dependency is needed only at runtime.
     - **Test**: The dependency is needed only for testing purposes.
3. **Ordering Dependencies**:
   - IntelliJ IDEA allows you to reorder dependencies to control their resolution order.
   - Use the Up and Down buttons in the Dependencies tab to change the order of dependencies.

Managing External Library Dependencies

External library dependencies are third-party libraries or frameworks that your project relies on. These dependencies can be managed through build tools like Maven and Gradle, or added manually.

1. **Adding External Libraries via Maven**:
   - Open the pom.xml file.
   - Add the required dependencies under the <dependencies> section.

```xml
Copy code
<dependency>
<groupId>org.example</groupId>
<artifactId>example-library</artifactId>
<version>1.0.0</version>
</dependency>
```

- o IntelliJ IDEA will automatically download and add the specified libraries to your project.

2. **Adding External Libraries via Gradle**:
    - o Open the build.gradle file.
    - o Add the required dependencies under the dependencies section.

```gradle
Copy code
dependencies {
    implementation 'org.example:example-library:1.0.0'
}
```

- o IntelliJ IDEA will automatically download and add the specified libraries to your project.

3. **Manually Adding External Libraries**:
    - o Go to File > Project Structure > Libraries.
    - o Click the + button and choose the library type.
    - o Specify the library files (JARs, directories).
    - o Assign the library to the relevant modules.

Practical Example: Configuring a Java Project

Let's walk through a practical example of configuring a Java project with multiple modules and external library dependencies.

1. **Create a New Project**:
    - o Open IntelliJ IDEA and select File > New > Project.
    - o Choose Java and click Next.
    - o Enter the project name (MyJavaProject) and specify the project location.
    - o Click Finish.

2. **Add Modules**:
    - o Go to File > Project Structure > Modules.
    - o Click the + button to add a new module.
    - o Choose Java and follow the wizard to create a module named CoreModule.
    - o Repeat the process to create another module named WebModule.

3. **Configure Module Content Roots**:
    - o Select CoreModule and navigate to the Sources tab.

- Add content roots for source and test code directories (e.g., src/main/java, src/test/java).
- Repeat the process for WebModule.

4. **Add Module Dependencies**:
   - Select WebModule and navigate to the Dependencies tab.
   - Click the + button and choose Module Dependency.
   - Select CoreModule and click OK.
   - Ensure the dependency scope is set to Compile.

5. **Add External Libraries**:
   - Open the pom.xml file (assuming you're using Maven).
   - Add dependencies for external libraries:

```xml
Copy code
<dependencies>
<dependency>
<groupId>org.springframework</groupId>
<artifactId>spring-core</artifactId>
<version>5.3.8</version>
</dependency>
<dependency>
<groupId>org.springframework</groupId>
<artifactId>spring-web</artifactId>
<version>5.3.8</version>
</dependency>
</dependencies>
```

   - IntelliJ IDEA will download and configure the specified libraries.

6. **Review and Adjust Settings**:
   - Go to File > Project Structure > Modules.
   - Verify that the content roots, dependencies, and module settings are correctly configured for both CoreModule and WebModule.

Practical Example: Configuring a Kotlin Project with Gradle

Next, let's configure a Kotlin project with Gradle, multiple modules, and external library dependencies.

1. **Create a New Project**:
   - Open IntelliJ IDEA and select File > New > Project.
   - Choose Kotlin > Kotlin/JVM and click Next.
   - Enter the project name (MyKotlinProject) and specify the project location.
   - Click Finish.

2. **Add Modules**:
   - Go to File > Project Structure > Modules.
   - Click the + button to add a new module.
   - Choose Kotlin and follow the wizard to create a module named ServiceModule.
   - Repeat the process to create another module named ApiModule.

3. **Configure Module Content Roots**:
   - Select ServiceModule and navigate to the Sources tab.
   - Add content roots for source and test code directories (e.g., src/main/kotlin, src/test/kotlin).
   - Repeat the process for ApiModule.

4. **Add Module Dependencies**:
   - Select ApiModule and navigate to the Dependencies tab.
   - Click the + button and choose Module Dependency.
   - Select ServiceModule and click OK.
   - Ensure the dependency scope is set to Compile.

5. **Add External Libraries**:
   - Open the build.gradle file (assuming you're using Gradle).
   - Add dependencies for external libraries:

```gradle
Copy code
dependencies {
    implementation 'org.jetbrains.kotlin:kotlin-stdlib:1.5.21'
    implementation 'com.squareup.okhttp3:okhttp:4.9.1'
}
```

   - IntelliJ IDEA will download and configure the specified libraries.

6. **Review and Adjust Settings**:
   - Go to File > Project Structure > Modules.

o Verify that the content roots, dependencies, and module settings are correctly configured for both ServiceModule and ApiModule.

Conclusion

Managing project structures in IntelliJ IDEA involves understanding the distinction between projects and modules, configuring project settings, and managing dependencies. By effectively organizing your project and its modules, you can streamline your development workflow, ensure code modularity, and maintain a clean and efficient codebase. IntelliJ IDEA's robust tools for configuring project structures and managing dependencies make it an ideal choice for handling complex projects with multiple modules and external libraries. With the knowledge gained from this chapter, you are well-equipped to create and manage well-structured projects in IntelliJ IDEA, ensuring a smooth and productive development experience.

2.4 Working with Version Control Systems

Version Control Systems (VCS) are integral to modern software development, enabling teams to collaborate efficiently and maintain a history of their codebase. IntelliJ IDEA supports various VCSs, including Git, SVN, Mercurial, and Perforce. This chapter will guide you through setting up a VCS in IntelliJ IDEA, performing basic VCS operations, and managing branches and merges.

Setting Up VCS

Setting up a VCS in IntelliJ IDEA involves configuring your project to work with your chosen version control system. Here, we'll focus on Git, the most widely used VCS. The steps for other VCSs are similar, with minor variations.

Configuring Git in IntelliJ IDEA

1. **Install Git**:
   o Ensure Git is installed on your system. You can download it from git-scm.com.
2. **Set Up Git in IntelliJ IDEA**:
   o Open IntelliJ IDEA and navigate to File > Settings (or IntelliJ IDEA > Preferences on macOS).

- o Go to Version Control > Git.
- o Ensure the Path to Git executable is correct. If it's not automatically detected, browse to the location where Git is installed.

3. **Clone a Repository**:
   - o Go to File > New > Project from Version Control.
   - o Select Git and enter the repository URL. Choose the directory where you want to clone the repository.
   - o Click Clone.

4. **Initialize a Repository**:
   - o To initialize a new Git repository, open your project in IntelliJ IDEA.
   - o Navigate to VCS > Import into Version Control > Create Git Repository.
   - o Select the root directory of your project and click OK.

Basic VCS Operations

Once you have set up Git, you can perform various VCS operations directly within IntelliJ IDEA. These operations include committing changes, pushing updates to a remote repository, and pulling updates from a remote repository.

Commit

Committing changes is the process of saving your work to the local repository. A commit is a snapshot of your project at a given point in time.

1. **Make Changes**:
   - o Modify your files as needed. IntelliJ IDEA will highlight changes in the editor and the Project tool window.

2. **Open the Commit Dialog**:
   - o Navigate to VCS > Commit or use the shortcut Ctrl+K (Windows/Linux) or Cmd+K (macOS).

3. **Select Changes**:
   - o In the Commit dialog, select the files you want to commit. IntelliJ IDEA will display the changes in a diff view.

4. **Enter a Commit Message**:
   - o Provide a meaningful commit message that describes your changes.

5. **Commit Changes**:
   - o Click Commit to save your changes to the local repository.

- Alternatively, you can choose Commit and Push to immediately push your changes to a remote repository.

Push

Pushing changes sends your commits from the local repository to a remote repository, making them available to other team members.

1. **Open the Push Dialog**:
   - Navigate to VCS > Git > Push or use the shortcut Ctrl+Shift+K (Windows/Linux) or Cmd+Shift+K (macOS).
2. **Select Changes**:
   - The Push dialog will display your local commits that are ready to be pushed.
3. **Push Changes**:
   - Click Push to send your commits to the remote repository.

Pull

Pulling changes fetches updates from a remote repository and merges them into your local repository.

1. **Open the Pull Dialog**:
   - Navigate to VCS > Git > Pull or use the shortcut Ctrl+T (Windows/Linux) or Cmd+T (macOS).
2. **Configure Pull Options**:
   - In the Pull dialog, you can select options such as Rebase or Merge to control how the updates are applied.
3. **Pull Changes**:
   - Click Pull to fetch and merge the updates from the remote repository.

Branching and Merging

Branches allow you to work on different features or fixes in isolation from the main codebase. Merging integrates changes from one branch into another.

Creating and Switching Branches

1. **Create a New Branch**:

- o   Open the Git tool window.
- o   Click the + button or navigate to VCS > Git > Branches > New Branch.
- o   Enter a branch name and click Create.

2. **Switch to a Branch**:
   - o   Open the Git tool window.
   - o   Click the current branch name to open the branch list.
   - o   Select the branch you want to switch to.

Merging Branches

Merging combines changes from one branch into another. This is commonly done to integrate feature branches into the main branch.

1. **Open the Git Tool Window**:
   - o   Navigate to VCS > Git > Branches.
2. **Select the Branch to Merge Into**:
   - o   Switch to the branch you want to merge into (e.g., main).
3. **Merge a Branch**:
   - o   In the Git tool window, click the current branch name to open the branch list.
   - o   Select Merge into Current and choose the branch you want to merge.
4. **Resolve Conflicts**:
   - o   If there are conflicts, IntelliJ IDEA will prompt you to resolve them.
   - o   Use the built-in merge tool to resolve conflicts by choosing changes from either branch or combining them manually.
5. **Complete the Merge**:
   - o   Once all conflicts are resolved, complete the merge process and commit the merged changes if necessary.

Practical Example: Basic VCS Operations with Git

Let's walk through a practical example of performing basic VCS operations using Git in IntelliJ IDEA.

Scenario: Working on a New Feature

1. **Create a New Branch**:
   - o   Open the Git tool window and create a new branch named feature/new-feature.
2. **Make Changes**:

- o Modify your project files to implement the new feature.
- o IntelliJ IDEA will highlight the changes in the editor and the Project tool window.

3. **Commit Changes**:
   - o Open the Commit dialog (Ctrl+K or Cmd+K).
   - o Select the modified files, enter a commit message (Implement new feature), and click Commit.

4. **Push Changes**:
   - o Open the Push dialog (Ctrl+Shift+K or Cmd+Shift+K).
   - o Select the local commits and click Push to send them to the remote repository.

5. **Switch to Main Branch**:
   - o Open the Git tool window and switch to the main branch.

6. **Merge Feature Branch**:
   - o Open the Git tool window, select main, and choose Merge into Current.
   - o Select the feature/new-feature branch to merge the changes.
   - o Resolve any conflicts and complete the merge.

7. **Push Merged Changes**:
   - o Open the Push dialog and push the merged changes to the remote repository.

Practical Example: Advanced VCS Operations

Scenario: Handling a Hotfix

1. **Create a Hotfix Branch**:
   - o Open the Git tool window and create a new branch named hotfix/critical-bug.

2. **Make Hotfix Changes**:
   - o Modify your project files to fix the critical bug.
   - o IntelliJ IDEA will highlight the changes.

3. **Commit Hotfix Changes**:
   - o Open the Commit dialog, select the modified files, enter a commit message (Fix critical bug), and click Commit.

4. **Push Hotfix Changes**:
   - o Open the Push dialog and push the changes to the remote repository.

5. **Switch to Main Branch**:
   - o Open the Git tool window and switch to the main branch.

6. **Merge Hotfix Branch**:
   - o Open the Git tool window, select main, and choose Merge into Current.
   - o Select the hotfix/critical-bug branch to merge the changes.

o   Resolve any conflicts and complete the merge.
7. **Push Merged Changes**:
   o   Open the Push dialog and push the merged changes to the remote repository.
8. **Tag the Release**:
   o   Open the Git tool window and switch to the main branch.
   o   Navigate to VCS > Git > Tag and create a new tag (e.g., v1.0.1).
   o   Push the tag to the remote repository.

Conclusion

Working with version control systems in IntelliJ IDEA is a seamless experience that integrates powerful VCS operations directly into your development workflow. By setting up a VCS, performing basic operations like committing, pushing, and pulling, and managing branches and merges, you can maintain a robust and organized codebase. IntelliJ IDEA's intuitive interface and comprehensive VCS support make it an excellent choice for both individual developers and teams, ensuring efficient collaboration and version management. With the skills and knowledge gained from this chapter, you are well-equipped to leverage the full potential of VCS in IntelliJ IDEA, enhancing your productivity and code quality.

Chapter 3: Navigating and Understanding Code

Efficiently navigating and understanding code is crucial for any developer. IntelliJ IDEA offers a wide array of tools and features to help you quickly find and comprehend the different parts of your codebase. In this chapter, we'll delve into basic code navigation techniques, including navigating to classes, files, and symbols, using the Project view, and working with recent files and locations. Mastering these techniques will significantly boost your productivity and help you maintain a clear understanding of your project.

3.1 Basic Code Navigation

Navigating to Class, File, Symbol

IntelliJ IDEA provides powerful search and navigation capabilities that allow you to quickly locate classes, files, and symbols within your project. These features are designed to minimize the time spent on navigating your codebase and maximize your focus on actual coding.

Navigating to a Class

Navigating to a class in IntelliJ IDEA is straightforward and efficient. The IDE offers several ways to do this:

1. **Using the Navigate to Class Action**:
   o Press Ctrl+N (Windows/Linux) or Cmd+O (macOS) to open the "Navigate to Class" dialog.
   o Start typing the name of the class you want to navigate to. IntelliJ IDEA will provide a list of matching classes.
   o Use CamelCase or snake_case notation to quickly filter results (e.g., typing "HTC" to find "HttpClient").
2. **Using the Project View**:
   o Open the Project tool window by pressing Alt+1 (Windows/Linux) or Cmd+1 (macOS).

- Expand the project tree and locate the class you want to navigate to.
3. **Using the Search Everywhere Feature**:
    - Press Shift twice to open the Search Everywhere dialog.
    - Type the name of the class and select it from the list of search results.

Navigating to a File

IntelliJ IDEA also provides several methods to navigate to a file within your project:

1. **Using the Navigate to File Action**:
    - Press Ctrl+Shift+N (Windows/Linux) or Cmd+Shift+O (macOS) to open the "Navigate to File" dialog.
    - Start typing the name of the file. IntelliJ IDEA will show a list of matching files.
    - Use CamelCase or snake_case notation to quickly filter results.
2. **Using the Project View**:
    - Open the Project tool window and expand the project tree to locate the file you want to navigate to.
3. **Using the Search Everywhere Feature**:
    - Press Shift twice, type the name of the file, and select it from the list of search results.

Navigating to a Symbol

Symbols include variables, methods, and fields within your code. IntelliJ IDEA makes it easy to navigate to these symbols:

1. **Using the Navigate to Symbol Action**:
    - Press Ctrl+Alt+Shift+N (Windows/Linux) or Cmd+Option+O (macOS) to open the "Navigate to Symbol" dialog.
    - Start typing the name of the symbol. IntelliJ IDEA will list matching symbols.
2. **Using the Structure Tool Window**:
    - Open the Structure tool window by pressing Ctrl+F12 (Windows/Linux) or Cmd+F12 (macOS).

- o This window displays the structure of the current file, allowing you to navigate to any symbol within it.
3. **Using the Search Everywhere Feature**:
   - o Press Shift twice, type the name of the symbol, and select it from the search results.

Using the Project View

The Project view in IntelliJ IDEA is a powerful tool for navigating and managing your project's files and directories. It provides a structured view of your project, allowing you to quickly locate and open files.

Accessing the Project View

1. **Open the Project Tool Window**:
   - o Press Alt+1 (Windows/Linux) or Cmd+1 (macOS) to open the Project tool window.
   - o Alternatively, you can go to View > Tool Windows > Project.
2. **Explore Project Structure**:
   - o The Project view displays your project as a tree structure. Expand and collapse directories to navigate through your project's files and folders.

Customizing the Project View

IntelliJ IDEA allows you to customize the Project view to suit your preferences and needs:

1. **View Options**:
   - o Right-click within the Project tool window to access view options.
   - o Choose between different views such as Project, Packages, and Problems.
2. **Filter and Sort**:
   - o Use the toolbar at the top of the Project tool window to filter and sort items.
   - o Options include showing/hiding hidden files, sorting alphabetically, and flattening packages.

Quick Navigation

1. **Navigate to File**:
   - Press Ctrl+Shift+N (Windows/Linux) or Cmd+Shift+O (macOS) to quickly navigate to a file.
   - Start typing the file name and select it from the list.
2. **Navigate to Class**:
   - Press Ctrl+N (Windows/Linux) or Cmd+O (macOS) to quickly navigate to a class.
   - Start typing the class name and select it from the list.
3. **Navigate to Symbol**:
   - Press Ctrl+Alt+Shift+N (Windows/Linux) or Cmd+Option+O (macOS) to quickly navigate to a symbol.
   - Start typing the symbol name and select it from the list.

Recent Files and Locations

IntelliJ IDEA provides features to help you quickly access recently opened files and locations, ensuring you can easily return to your work.

Recent Files

1. **Open Recent Files**:
   - Press Ctrl+E (Windows/Linux) or Cmd+E (macOS) to open the Recent Files dialog.
   - This dialog displays a list of recently opened files.
2. **Navigate Recent Files**:
   - Use the arrow keys or type to filter the list and select a file.
   - Press Enter to open the selected file.

Recent Locations

1. **Open Recent Locations**:
   - Press Ctrl+Shift+E (Windows/Linux) or Cmd+Shift+E (macOS) to open the Recent Locations dialog.
   - This dialog displays a list of recently visited locations in your code, such as method definitions or lines you have edited.
2. **Navigate Recent Locations**:

- o Use the arrow keys or type to filter the list and select a location.
- o Press Enter to navigate to the selected location.

Navigation History

IntelliJ IDEA keeps track of your navigation history, allowing you to move back and forth between locations you've visited.

1. **Back and Forward Navigation**:
   - o Use Ctrl+Alt+Left and Ctrl+Alt+Right (Windows/Linux) or Cmd+Option+Left and Cmd+Option+Right (macOS) to navigate back and forth in your history.
2. **Navigate Back/Forward Actions**:
   - o You can also navigate back and forward using the toolbar buttons or the Navigate menu.

Practical Example: Basic Code Navigation

Let's walk through a practical example of navigating a Java project using the techniques discussed.

Scenario: Navigating a Java Project

1. **Open the Project**:
   - o Open IntelliJ IDEA and load your Java project.
2. **Navigate to a Class**:
   - o Press Ctrl+N (Windows/Linux) or Cmd+O (macOS).
   - o Start typing the name of the class (e.g., UserService).
   - o Select the class from the list and press Enter to open it.
3. **Navigate to a File**:
   - o Press Ctrl+Shift+N (Windows/Linux) or Cmd+Shift+O (macOS).
   - o Start typing the name of the file (e.g., application.properties).
   - o Select the file from the list and press Enter to open it.
4. **Navigate to a Symbol**:
   - o Press Ctrl+Alt+Shift+N (Windows/Linux) or Cmd+Option+O (macOS).
   - o Start typing the name of the symbol (e.g., getUser method).
   - o Select the symbol from the list and press Enter to navigate to its definition.

5. **Using Project View**:
    - Press Alt+1 (Windows/Linux) or Cmd+1 (macOS) to open the Project tool window.
    - Expand the src/main/java directory and navigate to the desired package.
    - Open the UserService.java file by double-clicking it.
6. **Recent Files**:
    - Press Ctrl+E (Windows/Linux) or Cmd+E (macOS).
    - Select a recently opened file from the list and press Enter to open it.
7. **Recent Locations**:
    - Press Ctrl+Shift+E (Windows/Linux) or Cmd+Shift+E (macOS).
    - Select a recently visited location in your code and press Enter to navigate to it.
8. **Back and Forward Navigation**:
    - Use Ctrl+Alt+Left and Ctrl+Alt+Right (Windows/Linux) or Cmd+Option+Left and Cmd+Option+Right (macOS) to navigate back and forth in your navigation history.

Practical Example: Advanced Code Navigation

Scenario: Understanding a Complex Codebase

1. **Search Everywhere**:
    - Press Shift twice to open the Search Everywhere dialog.
    - Type the name of a class, file, or symbol (e.g., OrderController) and select it from the search results.
2. **Navigating to Implementations**:
    - Place the cursor on a method or interface name.
    - Press Ctrl+Alt+B (Windows/Linux) or Cmd+Option+B (macOS) to navigate to its implementations.
3. **Navigating to Super Methods**:
    - Place the cursor on an overridden method.
    - Press Ctrl+U (Windows/Linux) or Cmd+U (macOS) to navigate to its super method.
4. **File Structure Popup**:
    - Press Ctrl+F12 (Windows/Linux) or Cmd+F12 (macOS) to open the File Structure popup.

- Navigate to a method or field within the current file.
5. **Navigating to Related Files**:
    - Use the Navigate > Related Symbol menu to find related files, such as test classes or XML configuration files.

Conclusion

Mastering code navigation in IntelliJ IDEA is essential for any developer working on complex projects. By leveraging the powerful navigation features provided by IntelliJ IDEA, you can quickly locate classes, files, and symbols, efficiently use the Project view, and make use of recent files and locations to streamline your workflow. Whether you're navigating a simple project or understanding a complex codebase, the techniques covered in this chapter will significantly enhance your productivity and code comprehension. With these skills, you're well-equipped to navigate and understand any project in IntelliJ IDEA, ensuring a smooth and efficient development experience.

3.2 Advanced Code Navigation Techniques

As you become more familiar with IntelliJ IDEA, you can start leveraging its advanced navigation techniques to further enhance your productivity and understanding of your codebase. In this section, we will explore advanced code navigation features such as navigating to related symbols, using hyperlinks in code, and managing bookmarks and favorites.

Navigate to Related Symbol

Navigating to related symbols is an invaluable feature in IntelliJ IDEA that allows you to jump between various related code elements, such as method declarations and their implementations, test classes and the classes they test, and many more. This feature helps you quickly explore relationships within your code, improving your comprehension and efficiency.

Using the Navigate to Related Symbol Feature

1. **Navigate to Implementation**:
    - Place your cursor on a method name, interface, or an abstract class.

- Press Ctrl+Alt+B (Windows/Linux) or Cmd+Option+B (macOS) to navigate to its implementations.
- IntelliJ IDEA will display a list of all implementations. Select the one you want to navigate to.

2. **Navigate to Declaration or Usages**:
   - Place your cursor on a method, variable, or class name.
   - Press Ctrl+B (Windows/Linux) or Cmd+B (macOS) to navigate to its declaration.
   - To find usages, press Alt+F7 (Windows/Linux) or Option+F7 (macOS). IntelliJ IDEA will display a list of all places where the symbol is used.

3. **Navigate to Test or Tested Code**:
   - Place your cursor on a class or method name.
   - Use Navigate > Test (no default shortcut) to navigate to the corresponding test class or method.
   - This feature works both ways: from the class/method to its test and from the test to the tested class/method.

4. **Navigate to Super Method**:
   - Place your cursor on an overridden method.
   - Press Ctrl+U (Windows/Linux) or Cmd+U (macOS) to navigate to its super method.

Practical Example: Navigating Related Symbols

Let's walk through a practical example where we navigate through various related symbols in a Java project.

1. **Open a Class with Inheritance**:
   - Open a class that extends another class or implements an interface, for example, UserServiceImpl.

2. **Navigate to Superclass**:
   - Place the cursor on the class name UserServiceImpl.
   - Press Ctrl+U (Windows/Linux) or Cmd+U (macOS) to navigate to its superclass or implemented interface.

3. **Navigate to Method Implementation**:
   - Place the cursor on an overridden method, such as createUser.

- o Press Ctrl+Alt+B (Windows/Linux) or Cmd+Option+B (macOS) to navigate to other implementations of this method.
4. **Find Method Usages**:
   - o Place the cursor on the createUser method name.
   - o Press Alt+F7 (Windows/Linux) or Option+F7 (macOS) to find all usages of this method across the project.

Hyperlinks in Code

IntelliJ IDEA automatically recognizes various elements in your code and provides hyperlinks to navigate to their definitions or related locations. This feature helps you quickly jump to relevant code sections without having to manually search for them.

Types of Hyperlinks

1. **Class and Method References**:
   - o Class names, method names, and other symbols are often highlighted as hyperlinks.
   - o Click on these hyperlinks to navigate to their definitions.
2. **Annotations and Javadoc Links**:
   - o Links within Javadoc comments and annotations are also recognized.
   - o Click on these links to navigate to the referenced documentation or source code.
3. **Error and Warning Links**:
   - o Errors and warnings in the code editor often include links to quickly navigate to the related code section or suggested fix.
   - o Click on these links to jump to the corresponding location.

Using Hyperlinks in Code

1. **Navigate via Hyperlinks**:
   - o Hover over a class name, method, or variable to see if it is highlighted as a hyperlink.
   - o Click on the hyperlink to navigate to its definition or related code.
2. **Javadoc Links**:
   - o Hover over a Javadoc link within a comment block.

o   Click on the link to navigate to the referenced documentation or source code.

3. **Error and Warning Links**:
   o   Review the error or warning message in the code editor.
   o   Click on the link provided within the message to navigate to the suggested fix or related location.

Practical Example: Using Hyperlinks in Code

Let's explore how to use hyperlinks to navigate through code and documentation in a Java project.

1. **Open a Class with Javadoc**:
   o   Open a class with comprehensive Javadoc comments, such as UserService.
2. **Navigate Javadoc Links**:
   o   Find a Javadoc link within the comment, for example, a link to another class or method.
   o   Click on the link to navigate to the referenced class or method.
3. **Navigate via Class and Method Hyperlinks**:
   o   Locate a class name, method, or variable that IntelliJ IDEA has highlighted as a hyperlink.
   o   Click on the hyperlink to navigate to its definition.
4. **Error and Warning Links**:
   o   Introduce a code error or warning intentionally.
   o   Observe the error or warning message in the code editor.
   o   Click on the link within the message to navigate to the suggested fix or related location.

Bookmarks and Favorites

Bookmarks and favorites in IntelliJ IDEA allow you to mark and organize important code sections for quick access. These features are particularly useful for large projects where you need to frequently navigate to specific parts of your code.

Bookmarks

Bookmarks help you mark specific lines or files in your project so you can easily return to them later.

1. **Add a Bookmark**:
   - Place the cursor on the line you want to bookmark.
   - Press F11 (Windows/Linux/macOS) to add a simple bookmark.
   - For a mnemonic bookmark, press Ctrl+F11 (Windows/Linux) or Cmd+F11 (macOS) and choose a number or letter to associate with the bookmark.

2. **Navigate Bookmarks**:
   - Press Shift+F11 (Windows/Linux/macOS) to open the Bookmarks dialog.
   - Select a bookmark and press Enter to navigate to it.
   - Use the corresponding number or letter (if mnemonic bookmarks are used) to quickly jump to the bookmark.

3. **Remove a Bookmark**:
   - Navigate to the bookmarked line and press F11 (Windows/Linux/macOS) to remove the bookmark.
   - Alternatively, use the Bookmarks dialog to manage and remove bookmarks.

Favorites

Favorites help you organize important files, classes, and methods into customizable lists for quick access.

1. **Add to Favorites**:
   - Right-click on a file, class, or method in the Project view or editor.
   - Select Add to Favorites and choose or create a favorites list.

2. **Manage Favorites**:
   - Open the Favorites tool window by pressing Alt+2 (Windows/Linux) or Cmd+2 (macOS).
   - Use the tool window to organize, rename, or remove items from your favorites lists.

3. **Navigate Favorites**:
   - Open the Favorites tool window and select an item to navigate to it.

Practical Example: Using Bookmarks and Favorites

Let's walk through a practical example of using bookmarks and favorites to manage important code sections in a Java project.

1. **Open a Class**:
   - Open a class file with several methods, such as UserService.
2. **Add Simple Bookmarks**:
   - Place the cursor on important methods or lines, such as the createUser method.
   - Press F11 to add a simple bookmark.
3. **Add Mnemonic Bookmarks**:
   - Place the cursor on another important method or line, such as the deleteUser method.
   - Press Ctrl+F11 (Windows/Linux) or Cmd+F11 (macOS) and choose a number or letter to create a mnemonic bookmark.
4. **Navigate Bookmarks**:
   - Press Shift+F11 to open the Bookmarks dialog.
   - Select a bookmark and press Enter to navigate to it.
   - Use the assigned number or letter to quickly jump to a mnemonic bookmark.
5. **Add to Favorites**:
   - Right-click on the UserService class in the Project view.
   - Select Add to Favorites and create a new favorites list named Important Classes.
6. **Manage Favorites**:
   - Open the Favorites tool window by pressing Alt+2 (Windows/Linux) or Cmd+2 (macOS).
   - Use the tool window to view and organize your favorites lists.
7. **Navigate Favorites**:
   - Select the UserService class from the Important Classes favorites list to navigate to it.

Conclusion

Advanced code navigation techniques in IntelliJ IDEA can significantly enhance your ability to understand and manage complex codebases. By mastering features such as navigating to related symbols, using hyperlinks in code, and managing bookmarks and favorites, you can streamline your workflow and maintain a clear understanding of your project structure. These advanced navigation techniques, combined with the basic navigation skills covered earlier, will make you a more efficient and effective developer, capable of tackling even the most intricate codebases with ease.

3.3 Understanding Code with Diagrams

Visualizing code through diagrams is an effective way to understand the structure, relationships, and flow within your codebase. IntelliJ IDEA provides powerful tools for creating and working with various types of diagrams, including UML class diagrams, dependency diagrams, and method call hierarchies. This chapter explores these features and demonstrates how they can be used to gain deeper insights into your code.

UML Class Diagrams

Unified Modeling Language (UML) class diagrams are a standard way to visualize the static structure of a system, showcasing the classes, their attributes, methods, and the relationships between them. IntelliJ IDEA provides robust support for generating and working with UML class diagrams directly within the IDE.

Creating UML Class Diagrams

1. **Generate UML Class Diagram**:
   - Right-click on a package or class in the Project view.
   - Select Diagrams > Show Diagram from the context menu.
   - IntelliJ IDEA will generate a UML class diagram for the selected package or class, displaying it in a new editor tab.
2. **Adding Elements to the Diagram**:
   - You can manually add classes, interfaces, and other elements to the diagram.
   - Right-click on the diagram background and select New > Class or New > Interface to add new elements.
   - Use drag-and-drop from the Project view to add existing classes to the diagram.
3. **Customizing the Diagram**:
   - Use the toolbar at the top of the diagram editor to customize the layout and appearance.

- Options include zooming, layout adjustments, and toggling various display settings (e.g., attributes, methods, relationships).

Working with UML Class Diagrams

1. **Exploring Relationships**:
   - UML class diagrams visually represent relationships between classes, such as inheritance (generalization), associations, and dependencies.
   - Hover over connectors to see details about the relationship, such as cardinality and navigability.
2. **Navigating Code from Diagrams**:
   - Double-click on a class or method in the diagram to navigate directly to its definition in the code editor.
   - Use right-click context menus on diagram elements to access additional navigation and refactoring options.
3. **Exporting Diagrams**:
   - Diagrams can be exported for use in documentation or presentations.
   - Right-click on the diagram background and select Export Diagram to save the diagram as an image file (e.g., PNG, SVG).

Practical Example: Creating and Using UML Class Diagrams

Let's walk through a practical example of generating and using a UML class diagram in a Java project.

1. **Generate a UML Class Diagram**:
   - Right-click on the com.example.service package in the Project view.
   - Select Diagrams > Show Diagram.
   - IntelliJ IDEA will generate a UML class diagram for the com.example.service package, displaying classes such as UserService, OrderService, and their related classes.
2. **Explore Relationships**:
   - Observe the inheritance relationship between AbstractService and its subclasses UserService and OrderService.
   - Hover over the connectors to see details about associations and dependencies.

3. **Navigate to Code**:
   - ○ Double-click on the UserService class in the diagram to open its definition in the code editor.
   - ○ Navigate back to the diagram and explore other classes and relationships.
4. **Export the Diagram**:
   - ○ Right-click on the diagram background and select Export Diagram.
   - ○ Save the diagram as a PNG file for inclusion in project documentation.

Dependency Diagrams

Dependency diagrams help you understand the dependencies and interactions between various modules and components within your project. These diagrams are particularly useful for analyzing the impact of changes and identifying potential areas of improvement.

Creating Dependency Diagrams

1. **Generate Dependency Diagram**:
   - ○ Right-click on a module or package in the Project view.
   - ○ Select Analyze > Analyze Dependencies.
   - ○ IntelliJ IDEA will generate a dependency diagram, displaying the dependencies between the selected module or package and others in the project.
2. **Customizing the Diagram**:
   - ○ Use the toolbar to customize the layout and appearance of the diagram.
   - ○ Options include zooming, layout adjustments, and toggling the visibility of certain dependency types (e.g., compile-time, runtime).

Working with Dependency Diagrams

1. **Analyzing Dependencies**:
   - ○ Dependency diagrams visually represent dependencies between modules and packages.
   - ○ Use the diagram to identify direct and transitive dependencies, circular dependencies, and potential areas for refactoring.
2. **Navigating Code from Diagrams**:

- Double-click on a module or package in the diagram to navigate directly to its definition or configuration in the code editor.
- Use right-click context menus on diagram elements to access additional navigation and refactoring options.

3. **Exporting Diagrams**:
   - Dependency diagrams can be exported for use in documentation or presentations.
   - Right-click on the diagram background and select Export Diagram to save the diagram as an image file (e.g., PNG, SVG).

Practical Example: Creating and Using Dependency Diagrams

Let's walk through a practical example of generating and using a dependency diagram in a Java project.

1. **Generate a Dependency Diagram**:
   - Right-click on the com.example module in the Project view.
   - Select Analyze > Analyze Dependencies.
   - IntelliJ IDEA will generate a dependency diagram for the com.example module, displaying its dependencies on other modules and external libraries.

2. **Analyze Dependencies**:
   - Observe the direct and transitive dependencies between com.example and other modules such as com.example.service and com.example.data.
   - Identify any circular dependencies that may need refactoring.

3. **Navigate to Code**:
   - Double-click on the com.example.service module in the diagram to open its definition or configuration in the code editor.
   - Navigate back to the diagram and explore other dependencies.

4. **Export the Diagram**:
   - Right-click on the diagram background and select Export Diagram.
   - Save the diagram as a PNG file for inclusion in project documentation.

Method Call Hierarchies

Understanding the flow of method calls within your code is crucial for comprehending complex logic and identifying potential issues. IntelliJ IDEA provides tools for visualizing and exploring method call hierarchies, making it easier to trace the execution flow and dependencies between methods.

Creating Method Call Hierarchies

1. **Generate Method Call Hierarchy**:
   - Place your cursor on a method in the code editor.
   - Press Ctrl+Alt+H (Windows/Linux) or Cmd+Option+H (macOS) to open the Method Call Hierarchy tool window.
   - IntelliJ IDEA will generate a hierarchy tree, displaying all methods that call or are called by the selected method.
2. **Customizing the Hierarchy View**:
   - Use the toolbar in the Method Call Hierarchy tool window to customize the view.
   - Options include toggling between caller and callee hierarchies, filtering by scope (e.g., project, module), and adjusting the display settings.

Working with Method Call Hierarchies

1. **Exploring the Hierarchy**:
   - Use the Method Call Hierarchy tool window to explore the hierarchy tree.
   - Expand and collapse nodes to see the full call hierarchy, tracing method calls from the selected method to its callers and callees.
2. **Navigating Code from Hierarchies**:
   - Double-click on a method in the hierarchy tree to navigate directly to its definition in the code editor.
   - Use right-click context menus on hierarchy elements to access additional navigation and refactoring options.
3. **Exporting Hierarchies**:
   - Method call hierarchies can be exported for use in documentation or presentations.
   - Use the Export to Text or Export to XML options in the Method Call Hierarchy tool window to save the hierarchy.

Practical Example: Creating and Using Method Call Hierarchies

Let's walk through a practical example of generating and using a method call hierarchy in a Java project.

1. **Generate a Method Call Hierarchy**:
   o Place your cursor on the createUser method in the UserService class.
   o Press Ctrl+Alt+H (Windows/Linux) or Cmd+Option+H (macOS) to open the Method Call Hierarchy tool window.
   o IntelliJ IDEA will generate a hierarchy tree, displaying all methods that call or are called by createUser.
2. **Explore the Hierarchy**:
   o Expand the nodes in the hierarchy tree to see the full call hierarchy.
   o Trace method calls from createUser to its callers and callees.
3. **Navigate to Code**:
   o Double-click on a method in the hierarchy tree, such as createUser's caller method registerUser.
   o Navigate back to the hierarchy and explore other methods.
4. **Export the Hierarchy**:
   o Use the Export to Text option in the Method Call Hierarchy tool window.
   o Save the hierarchy as a text file for inclusion in project documentation.

Conclusion

Understanding code through diagrams is a powerful technique that can greatly enhance your comprehension and management of complex codebases. IntelliJ IDEA provides robust support for creating and working with UML class diagrams, dependency diagrams, and method call hierarchies. By mastering these tools, you can gain deeper insights into your code, identify potential issues, and streamline your development workflow.

3.4 Using the Structure Tool Window

The Structure tool window in IntelliJ IDEA is an indispensable feature that allows you to view and navigate the structure of your classes and files efficiently. It provides a hierarchical view of the elements within a file, such as classes, methods, fields, and other members, making it easier to understand and manage your code. In this section, we will delve into the basics of the Structure view, explore how to navigate class and method structures, and discuss customization options to tailor the view to your needs.

Structure View Basics

The Structure tool window provides a detailed, tree-like representation of the elements in your current file, including classes, methods, fields, and more. This view helps you quickly locate and navigate to specific parts of your code, enhancing your productivity and code comprehension.

Accessing the Structure Tool Window

1. **Opening the Structure Tool Window**:
   - To open the Structure tool window, you can use the keyboard shortcut Alt+7 (Windows/Linux) or Cmd+7 (macOS).
   - Alternatively, you can open it from the main menu by selecting View > Tool Windows > Structure.
2. **Basic Layout**:
   - The Structure tool window typically appears on the left or right side of the IntelliJ IDEA window, depending on your configuration.
   - It displays a hierarchical view of the current file's structure, with expandable and collapsible nodes representing classes, methods, fields, and other elements.
3. **Element Icons**:
   - Each element in the Structure view is accompanied by an icon that represents its type (e.g., class, method, field).
   - These icons help you quickly identify the nature of each element at a glance.

Navigating the Structure Tool Window

1. **Selecting Elements**:
   - Click on any element in the Structure view to highlight it in the editor.
   - Double-click on an element to navigate directly to its definition in the code editor.

2. **Expanding and Collapsing Nodes**:
   - ○ Use the arrow icons or click on the node to expand or collapse its children.
   - ○ This feature helps you manage the visibility of elements, focusing only on the parts of the structure you are interested in.
3. **Filtering Elements**:
   - ○ The Structure tool window provides filtering options to narrow down the elements displayed.
   - ○ Use the filter icons in the toolbar to show or hide specific types of elements (e.g., inherited members, anonymous classes).

Navigating Class and Method Structure

The Structure tool window is particularly useful for navigating the class and method structures within your files. Understanding and efficiently navigating these structures can significantly enhance your productivity, especially when working with large and complex codebases.

Class Structure Navigation

1. **Viewing Class Members**:
   - ○ When you open a class file, the Structure tool window displays all members of the class, including fields, methods, constructors, and inner classes.
   - ○ Members are organized in a tree-like structure, reflecting their hierarchical relationships.
2. **Navigating to Fields and Methods**:
   - ○ Click on a field or method in the Structure view to highlight it in the editor.
   - ○ Double-click to navigate directly to the field or method's definition.
3. **Access Modifiers and Inheritance**:
   - ○ The icons next to each member indicate its access modifier (e.g., public, private, protected) and whether it is static or final.
   - ○ Inherited members from parent classes or interfaces are also displayed, helping you understand the full scope of the class.

Method Structure Navigation

1. **Viewing Method Elements**:
    - o The Structure tool window displays all elements within a method, including local variables, parameters, and nested blocks.
    - o This view helps you understand the internal structure and flow of the method.
2. **Navigating Method Blocks**:
    - o Click on a nested block or local variable to highlight it in the editor.
    - o Double-click to navigate directly to the code block or variable's definition.
3. **Anonymous Classes and Lambdas**:
    - o Anonymous classes and lambda expressions within methods are also displayed in the Structure view.
    - o Navigate to these elements to understand their implementation and relationship with the enclosing method.

Customizing Structure View

IntelliJ IDEA allows you to customize the Structure tool window to suit your preferences and workflow. Customization options include adjusting the display settings, filtering elements, and configuring the layout.

Adjusting Display Settings

1. **Show Members in Alphabetical Order**:
    - o By default, members are displayed in the order they appear in the code.
    - o To sort members alphabetically, click the Sort by Name icon in the toolbar.
2. **Show/Hide Visibility Icons**:
    - o Visibility icons (e.g., public, private) provide additional information about each member's access level.
    - o Toggle these icons on or off using the Show Visibility Icons option in the toolbar.
3. **Show Inherited Members**:
    - o By default, inherited members are displayed in the Structure view.
    - o You can toggle this option to show or hide inherited members using the Show Inherited Members icon in the toolbar.

Filtering Elements

1. **Filter by Element Type**:
   - The Structure tool window allows you to filter elements based on their type, such as fields, methods, constructors, and inner classes.
   - Use the filter icons in the toolbar to show or hide specific types of elements.
2. **Search Within Structure**:
   - The search bar at the top of the Structure tool window allows you to quickly find elements by name.
   - Type a partial or full name to filter the displayed elements and highlight matches.
3. **Filter by Visibility**:
   - You can filter elements based on their visibility (e.g., public, private).
   - Use the Visibility filter in the toolbar to show or hide elements with specific visibility modifiers.

Configuring Layout

1. **Docking and Floating**:
   - The Structure tool window can be docked to various sides of the IntelliJ IDEA window or set to float independently.
   - Right-click on the title bar of the Structure tool window and choose from options such as Dock Pinned, Dock Unpinned, Floating, or Windowed.
2. **Splitting Views**:
   - You can split the Structure tool window to view different parts of the structure simultaneously.
   - Right-click on the title bar and select Split Vertically or Split Horizontally to create a split view.
3. **Resizing and Collapsing**:
   - Adjust the size of the Structure tool window by dragging its borders.
   - Collapse or expand the tool window using the minimize/maximize icons in the title bar.

Practical Example: Using and Customizing the Structure Tool Window

Let's walk through a practical example of using and customizing the Structure tool window in a Java project.

1. **Open a Class File**:
   - o Open the UserService class file in the code editor.
   - o The Structure tool window will automatically display the members of the UserService class.
2. **Navigate Class Members**:
   - o Click on the createUser method in the Structure view to highlight it in the editor.
   - o Double-click to navigate directly to the createUser method's definition.
3. **Customize Display Settings**:
   - o Click the Sort by Name icon in the toolbar to sort members alphabetically.
   - o Toggle the Show Visibility Icons option to display or hide access modifier icons.
4. **Filter Elements**:
   - o Use the filter icons in the toolbar to hide all fields, showing only methods and inner classes.
   - o Type deleteUser in the search bar to quickly find and highlight the deleteUser method.
5. **Configure Layout**:
   - o Right-click on the title bar of the Structure tool window and select Split Vertically to create a split view.
   - o Adjust the size of the Structure tool window by dragging its borders.
6. **Navigate Method Elements**:
   - o Click on a local variable within the createUser method to highlight it in the editor.
   - o Double-click to navigate directly to the variable's definition.

Conclusion

The Structure tool window in IntelliJ IDEA is a powerful feature that provides a detailed, hierarchical view of the elements within your files. By mastering the use of this tool, you can significantly enhance your ability to navigate and understand complex code structures, improving your productivity and code comprehension.

In this chapter, we explored the basics of the Structure tool window, including how to access and navigate it. We also discussed advanced techniques for navigating class and method structures and customizing the Structure view to suit your preferences. By leveraging these features, you can streamline your workflow and maintain a clear understanding of your project's structure, ensuring a more efficient and effective development experience.

Chapter 4: Writing and Editing Code

4.1 Code Completion and Suggestions

IntelliJ IDEA offers a comprehensive suite of code completion features that enhance productivity and code quality. These features include basic completion, smart completion, postfix completion, and live templates. Understanding how to leverage these tools effectively can significantly streamline your coding process and reduce errors.

Basic Completion vs. Smart Completion

IntelliJ IDEA provides two primary types of code completion: basic completion and smart completion. Each serves different purposes and can be used in different scenarios to assist you in writing code more efficiently.

Basic Completion

Basic completion provides a list of all available symbols that are accessible within the current context. It is a broad tool that helps you quickly find and insert the names of classes, methods, fields, and keywords.

1. **Invoking Basic Completion**:
   - Press Ctrl+Space (Windows/Linux) or Cmd+Space (macOS) to invoke basic completion.
   - IntelliJ IDEA will display a list of all symbols that are relevant in the current context.
2. **Usage Scenarios**:
   - Basic completion is ideal when you need to quickly insert a symbol whose name you partially remember.
   - It is useful for completing class names, method names, variable names, and keywords.
3. **Example**:

- Suppose you are writing a method in a class and need to call another method, calculateTotal. Start typing calc, press Ctrl+Space, and select calculateTotal from the list of suggestions.

Smart Completion

Smart completion provides context-aware suggestions by considering the expected type of the expression and the current scope. This feature is more precise than basic completion and can significantly reduce the time spent searching for the correct symbol.

1. **Invoking Smart Completion**:
   - Press Ctrl+Shift+Space (Windows/Linux) or Cmd+Shift+Space (macOS) to invoke smart completion.
   - IntelliJ IDEA will display a list of symbols that are most relevant based on the expected type and context.
2. **Usage Scenarios**:
   - Smart completion is ideal when you need more specific suggestions that match the expected type of an expression.
   - It is useful for completing method calls, variable assignments, and initializing objects.
3. **Example**:
   - Suppose you are assigning a value to a variable of type List<String>. Start typing the variable name, press Ctrl+Shift+Space, and select an appropriate method that returns a List<String> from the list of suggestions.

Postfix Completion

Postfix completion is a unique feature in IntelliJ IDEA that allows you to transform an existing expression by appending a postfix. This feature can save you time by eliminating the need to move the cursor back and forth within the code.

1. **Using Postfix Completion**:
   - Type an expression followed by a dot and a postfix.
   - Press Tab to apply the postfix completion, transforming the expression accordingly.
2. **Available Postfixes**:

- o Common postfixes include .if, .var, .not, .for, and .null.
- o These postfixes help you quickly create control flow statements, variable declarations, and other common code constructs.

3. **Example**:
   - o Suppose you have a boolean expression isValid and want to create an if statement. Type isValid.if, press Tab, and IntelliJ IDEA will transform it into if (isValid) { }, placing the cursor inside the braces.

Live Templates for Reusable Code

Live templates are predefined code snippets that can be quickly inserted into your code. They help you write common code constructs more efficiently and consistently. IntelliJ IDEA provides a wide range of built-in live templates, and you can also create your own custom templates.

Using Live Templates

1. **Invoking Live Templates**:
   - o Type the abbreviation of a live template and press Tab to insert the template.
   - o Alternatively, press Ctrl+J (Windows/Linux) or Cmd+J (macOS) to display a list of available live templates.

2. **Common Live Templates**:
   - o sout: Inserts System.out.println().
   - o psvm: Inserts the main method declaration public static void main(String[] args) { }.
   - o fori: Inserts a standard for loop.

3. **Example**:
   - o Type psvm in a class file and press Tab to insert the main method declaration. IntelliJ IDEA will automatically position the cursor inside the method body, ready for you to start writing code.

Creating Custom Live Templates

1. **Accessing Live Template Settings**:

o Go to File > Settings > Editor > Live Templates (Windows/Linux) or IntelliJ IDEA > Preferences > Editor > Live Templates (macOS).

2. **Creating a New Template**:
   - o Click on the + icon to create a new live template.
   - o Enter an abbreviation, a description, and the template text.

3. **Defining Variables**:
   - o Use VAR syntax to define variables within the template.
   - o Specify default values and expressions for variables to control their behavior.

4. **Example**:
   - o Create a custom live template for a logging statement. Use the abbreviation log, description Log statement, and template text logger.info("$MESSAGE$");. Define $MESSAGE$ as a variable with a default value of message.

Practical Examples

Let's walk through some practical examples of using these code completion features in a Java project.

Example 1: Basic Completion

1. **Scenario**:
   - o You are writing a method to process user data and need to call a method getUserInfo.

2. **Steps**:
   - o Start typing getUser.
   - o Press Ctrl+Space to invoke basic completion.
   - o Select getUserInfo from the list of suggestions.

Example 2: Smart Completion

1. **Scenario**:
   - o You are assigning a value to a Map<String, Integer> variable and need to find a method that returns a compatible type.

2. **Steps**:

- Start typing the variable name, followed by an equals sign.
- Press Ctrl+Shift+Space to invoke smart completion.
- Select an appropriate method that returns a Map<String, Integer> from the list of suggestions.

Example 3: Postfix Completion

1. **Scenario**:
   - You have an expression userList and want to iterate over it using a for loop.
2. **Steps**:
   - Type userList.for.
   - Press Tab to apply postfix completion.
   - IntelliJ IDEA will transform it into a for loop: for (User user : userList) { }.

Example 4: Using Live Templates

1. **Scenario**:
   - You need to insert a main method in a new class.
2. **Steps**:
   - Type psvm in the class file.
   - Press Tab to insert the main method declaration.

Example 5: Creating a Custom Live Template

1. **Scenario**:
   - You frequently write log statements and want to create a custom live template.
2. **Steps**:
   - Go to File > Settings > Editor > Live Templates.
   - Click on the + icon to create a new live template.
   - Enter log as the abbreviation, Log statement as the description, and logger.info("$MESSAGE$"); as the template text.
   - Define $MESSAGE$ as a variable with a default value of message.
3. **Usage**:
   - Type log in your code and press Tab to insert the log statement template.
   - Replace $MESSAGE$ with the actual log message.

4.2 Code Snippets and Templates

IntelliJ IDEA provides robust support for code snippets and templates, enabling you to write code more efficiently and consistently. Custom templates, surround with templates, and effective management of code snippets are powerful tools that can significantly streamline your development process. In this chapter, we will explore how to create and use custom templates, leverage surround with templates, and manage code snippets effectively.

Creating and Using Custom Templates

Custom templates in IntelliJ IDEA allow you to define reusable code snippets that can be quickly inserted into your codebase. This feature is particularly useful for inserting repetitive code structures and ensuring consistency across your projects.

Creating Custom Templates

1. **Accessing Live Template Settings**:
   - Navigate to File > Settings > Editor > Live Templates (Windows/Linux) or IntelliJ IDEA > Preferences > Editor > Live Templates (macOS).
2. **Creating a New Template**:
   - Click the + icon to create a new live template.
   - Enter an abbreviation that you will use to invoke the template.
   - Provide a description to explain the purpose of the template.
   - In the template text area, enter the code snippet you want to reuse.
3. **Defining Variables**:
   - Use the VAR syntax to define variables within the template.
   - Variables can have default values or expressions that generate their values.
   - Define the scope and expressions for each variable to control how they behave when the template is expanded.
4. **Example**:
   - Create a custom template for a logging statement:
     - Abbreviation: log
     - Description: Log statement
     - Template text: logger.info("$MESSAGE$");

- Define $MESSAGE$ as a variable with a default value of message.

Using Custom Templates

1. **Inserting a Template**:
   - Type the abbreviation of the template in the editor and press Tab to expand it.
   - Alternatively, press Ctrl+J (Windows/Linux) or Cmd+J (macOS) to open the list of available live templates and select the desired template.

2. **Example Usage**:
   - Type log in your code and press Tab to insert the logging statement template.
   - Replace $MESSAGE$ with the actual log message.

3. **Template Variables**:
   - When you expand a template, IntelliJ IDEA highlights the variables and allows you to replace them with actual values.
   - Use the Tab key to navigate between variables and fill in the necessary details.

Surround With Templates

Surround with templates are a convenient way to wrap existing code with predefined code structures, such as loops, conditionals, and try-catch blocks. This feature can help you quickly apply common programming patterns to your code.

Using Surround With Templates

1. **Selecting Code**:
   - Select the code you want to surround with a template.

2. **Invoking Surround With**:
   - Press Ctrl+Alt+T (Windows/Linux) or Cmd+Alt+T (macOS) to open the surround with menu.
   - Choose the desired template from the list.

3. **Example Usage**:
   - Select a block of code that needs to be wrapped in a try-catch block.
   - Press Ctrl+Alt+T (Windows/Linux) or Cmd+Alt+T (macOS) and choose try-catch.

- IntelliJ IDEA will wrap the selected code in a try-catch block and place the cursor inside the catch block for you to handle the exception.

Customizing Surround With Templates

1. **Creating Custom Surround Templates**:
   - Go to File > Settings > Editor > Live Templates.
   - Create a new template under a suitable context (e.g., Java).
   - Use predefined variables and template syntax to define the structure of the surrounding code.
2. **Example**:
   - Create a custom surround template for logging method entry and exit:
     - Abbreviation: logMethod
     - Description: Log method entry and exit
     - Template text:

```java
Copy code
logger.info("Entering method $METHOD$()");
$SELECTION$
logger.info("Exiting method $METHOD$()");
```

Managing Code Snippets

Managing code snippets efficiently involves organizing, importing, and sharing your templates to ensure consistency and reuse across different projects and team members.

Organizing Code Snippets

1. **Grouping Templates**:
   - In the live templates settings, organize your templates into groups based on their context (e.g., Java, XML, HTML).
   - This helps you quickly find and use the appropriate templates for different types of code.
2. **Example Groups**:
   - Create groups for commonly used templates in your projects, such as Logging, Database, Testing, and Utilities.

3. **Renaming and Deleting Templates**:
   - Right-click on a template to rename or delete it.
   - Use meaningful names and descriptions to make templates easy to understand and use.

Importing and Exporting Templates

1. **Exporting Templates**:
   - To share your templates with team members, you can export them to a file.
   - In the live templates settings, select the templates you want to export and click the Export button.
   - Save the templates to an XML file.
2. **Importing Templates**:
   - To import templates, click the Import button in the live templates settings.
   - Select the XML file containing the templates and import them into your IntelliJ IDEA installation.
3. **Example**:
   - Export your custom logging templates and share them with your team.
   - Team members can import the templates to ensure consistent logging practices across the project.

Sharing Templates Across Projects

1. **Project-Level Templates**:
   - Store templates in the .idea directory of your project to make them available to all team members working on the same project.
2. **Global Templates**:
   - For templates that should be available across all projects, configure them in the IDE settings rather than at the project level.
3. **Example**:
   - Create a set of templates for common database operations and store them in your project's .idea directory.
   - All team members will have access to these templates, ensuring consistency in database interaction code.

Practical Examples

Let's explore practical examples of using and managing code snippets and templates in a Java project.

Example 1: Creating and Using a Custom Template

1. **Scenario**:
   - You frequently write code to create and configure HTTP clients and want to create a reusable template for this.
2. **Steps**:
   - Go to File > Settings > Editor > Live Templates.
   - Create a new template with the abbreviation httpClient.
   - Provide a description: Create and configure HTTP client.
   - Template text:

     ```java
     Copy code
     HttpClient client = HttpClient.newBuilder()
     .version(HttpClient.Version.HTTP_2)
     .connectTimeout(Duration.ofSeconds($TIMEOUT$))
     .build();
     ```

   - Define $TIMEOUT$ as a variable with a default value of 10.
3. **Usage**:
   - Type httpClient in your code and press Tab to insert the HTTP client creation code.
   - Replace $TIMEOUT$ with the desired timeout value.

Example 2: Using Surround With Templates

1. **Scenario**:
   - You have a block of code that requires exception handling using a try-catch block.
2. **Steps**:
   - Select the block of code that needs to be wrapped in a try-catch block.
   - Press Ctrl+Alt+T (Windows/Linux) or Cmd+Alt+T (macOS) and choose try-catch.

92

o   IntelliJ IDEA will wrap the selected code in a try-catch block and place the cursor inside the catch block.

Example 3: Managing and Sharing Code Snippets

1. **Scenario**:
    o   You have created a set of custom templates for logging and want to share them with your team.
2. **Steps**:
    o   Go to File > Settings > Editor > Live Templates.
    o   Select the logging templates you want to share.
    o   Click the Export button and save the templates to an XML file.
    o   Share the XML file with your team members.
3. **Importing Templates**:
    o   Team members can import the templates by going to File > Settings > Editor > Live Templates.
    o   Click the Import button and select the XML file containing the templates.

4.3 Refactoring Tools

Refactoring is a critical part of software development that involves restructuring existing code without changing its external behavior. IntelliJ IDEA offers a comprehensive set of refactoring tools that make it easy to clean up your code, improve its readability, and maintainability. This chapter explores the refactoring tools available in IntelliJ IDEA, including renaming and safe delete, extract method, variable, and constant, as well as refactorings for classes and interfaces.

Renaming and Safe Delete

Renaming and safe delete are essential refactoring tools that help you maintain the integrity of your codebase while making necessary changes. These tools ensure that all references to a symbol are updated or removed correctly, preventing errors and improving code readability.

Renaming

Renaming is one of the most commonly used refactoring operations. It allows you to change the name of variables, methods, classes, and other symbols consistently across your codebase.

1. **Using Rename Refactoring**:
   - Select the symbol you want to rename (e.g., a variable, method, class).
   - Press Shift+F6 to open the rename dialog.
   - Enter the new name and press Enter.

2. **Example**:
   - Suppose you have a variable count that you want to rename to totalCount. Select the variable, press Shift+F6, enter totalCount, and press Enter. IntelliJ IDEA will update all references to this variable throughout the codebase.

3. **Previewing Changes**:
   - IntelliJ IDEA provides a preview of the changes before applying them.
   - This preview helps you review the changes and ensure that they do not introduce any issues.

4. **Renaming Across Files**:
   - The rename refactoring tool updates references across all files in the project.
   - This ensures consistency and prevents broken references.

Safe Delete

Safe delete ensures that you can remove a symbol (e.g., a variable, method, class) without breaking the code. IntelliJ IDEA checks for references to the symbol and warns you if it is still in use.

1. **Using Safe Delete**:
   - Select the symbol you want to delete.
   - Press Alt+Delete to open the safe delete dialog.
   - IntelliJ IDEA will check for references to the symbol and display a warning if it is still in use.

2. **Example**:
   - Suppose you want to delete a method calculateTotal. Select the method, press Alt+Delete, and IntelliJ IDEA will check for references to this method. If

the method is still in use, IntelliJ IDEA will warn you and provide the option to review the references.

3. **Previewing Changes**:
   - IntelliJ IDEA provides a preview of the changes before applying them.
   - This preview helps you review the changes and ensure that they do not introduce any issues.

4. **Handling References**:
   - If there are references to the symbol being deleted, IntelliJ IDEA provides options to update or remove these references.
   - This ensures that the code remains consistent and free of errors.

Extract Method, Variable, Constant

Extract refactorings are used to create new methods, variables, or constants from existing code. These refactorings help you break down complex code into smaller, more manageable pieces, improving readability and maintainability.

Extract Method

Extract method is used to create a new method from a block of code. This refactoring is useful for breaking down large methods into smaller, more focused methods.

1. **Using Extract Method**:
   - Select the block of code you want to extract.
   - Press Ctrl+Alt+M (Windows/Linux) or Cmd+Alt+M (macOS) to open the extract method dialog.
   - Enter the name of the new method and press Enter.

2. **Example**:
   - Suppose you have a block of code that calculates the total price in a method. Select the block of code, press Ctrl+Alt+M, enter calculateTotalPrice, and press Enter. IntelliJ IDEA will create a new method calculateTotalPrice and replace the selected code with a call to this method.

3. **Parameter Handling**:
   - IntelliJ IDEA automatically detects variables used in the selected code block and adds them as parameters to the new method.
   - This ensures that the new method has access to all the necessary data.

4. **Method Visibility**:
   - ○ You can set the visibility (public, private, protected) of the new method in the extract method dialog.
   - ○ This helps you control the scope of the new method.

Extract Variable

Extract variable is used to create a new variable from an expression. This refactoring is useful for simplifying complex expressions and improving code readability.

1. **Using Extract Variable**:
   - ○ Select the expression you want to extract.
   - ○ Press Ctrl+Alt+V (Windows/Linux) or Cmd+Alt+V (macOS) to open the extract variable dialog.
   - ○ Enter the name of the new variable and press Enter.
2. **Example**:
   - ○ Suppose you have a complex expression price * quantity in your code. Select the expression, press Ctrl+Alt+V, enter totalPrice, and press Enter. IntelliJ IDEA will create a new variable totalPrice and replace the selected expression with this variable.
3. **Variable Type**:
   - ○ IntelliJ IDEA automatically detects the type of the new variable.
   - ○ This ensures that the variable is declared with the correct type.
4. **Scope**:
   - ○ You can set the scope (local, field) of the new variable in the extract variable dialog.
   - ○ This helps you control where the new variable can be used.

Extract Constant

Extract constant is used to create a new constant from a literal value. This refactoring is useful for replacing magic numbers and strings with named constants, improving code readability and maintainability.

1. **Using Extract Constant**:
   - ○ Select the literal value you want to extract.

- o Press Ctrl+Alt+C (Windows/Linux) or Cmd+Alt+C (macOS) to open the extract constant dialog.
- o Enter the name of the new constant and press Enter.

2. **Example**:
   - o Suppose you have a literal value 3.14 in your code. Select the value, press Ctrl+Alt+C, enter PI, and press Enter. IntelliJ IDEA will create a new constant PI and replace the selected value with this constant.

3. **Constant Type**:
   - o IntelliJ IDEA automatically detects the type of the new constant.
   - o This ensures that the constant is declared with the correct type.

4. **Visibility**:
   - o You can set the visibility (public, private, protected) of the new constant in the extract constant dialog.
   - o This helps you control the scope of the new constant.

Refactorings for Classes and Interfaces

Refactorings for classes and interfaces help you restructure your codebase by moving, renaming, and modifying classes and interfaces. These refactorings improve code organization, readability, and maintainability.

Renaming Classes and Interfaces

Renaming classes and interfaces is similar to renaming other symbols. IntelliJ IDEA updates all references to the renamed class or interface, ensuring consistency across the codebase.

1. **Using Rename Refactoring**:
   - o Select the class or interface you want to rename.
   - o Press Shift+F6 to open the rename dialog.
   - o Enter the new name and press Enter.

2. **Example**:
   - o Suppose you have a class User that you want to rename to Customer. Select the class, press Shift+F6, enter Customer, and press Enter. IntelliJ IDEA will update all references to this class throughout the codebase.

3. **Previewing Changes**:

- o IntelliJ IDEA provides a preview of the changes before applying them.
- o This preview helps you review the changes and ensure that they do not introduce any issues.

4. **Renaming Across Files**:
   - o The rename refactoring tool updates references across all files in the project.
   - o This ensures consistency and prevents broken references.

Moving Classes and Interfaces

Moving classes and interfaces involves changing their location within the project. IntelliJ IDEA updates all references to the moved class or interface, ensuring consistency across the codebase.

1. **Using Move Refactoring**:
   - o Select the class or interface you want to move.
   - o Press F6 to open the move dialog.
   - o Choose the new package or directory and press Enter.
2. **Example**:
   - o Suppose you have a class User in the package com.example.model that you want to move to com.example.entity. Select the class, press F6, choose the new package, and press Enter. IntelliJ IDEA will move the class and update all references to it throughout the codebase.
3. **Previewing Changes**:
   - o IntelliJ IDEA provides a preview of the changes before applying them.
   - o This preview helps you review the changes and ensure that they do not introduce any issues.
4. **Moving Across Modules**:
   - o The move refactoring tool supports moving classes and interfaces across different modules in the project.
   - o This helps you reorganize your codebase as needed.

Extract Interface

Extract interface is a refactoring that creates a new interface from an existing class. This refactoring is useful for defining common behavior and decoupling implementations from interfaces.

1. **Using Extract Interface**:
   - Select the class from which you want to extract an interface.
   - Press Ctrl+Alt+Shift+T (Windows/Linux) or Cmd+Alt+Shift+T (macOS) and choose Extract Interface.
   - Select the methods to be included in the new interface and press Enter.

2. **Example**:
   - Suppose you have a class UserService with several methods. You want to extract an interface UserService to define the contract for this class. Select the class, press Ctrl+Alt+Shift+T, choose Extract Interface, select the methods to include, and press Enter. IntelliJ IDEA will create the interface and update the class to implement it.

3. **Interface Visibility**:
   - You can set the visibility (public, private, protected) of the new interface in the extract interface dialog.
   - This helps you control the scope of the new interface.

4. **Implementing Classes**:
   - IntelliJ IDEA automatically updates the class to implement the new interface.
   - This ensures that the class conforms to the contract defined by the interface.

Extract Superclass

Extract superclass is a refactoring that creates a new superclass from an existing class. This refactoring is useful for promoting common behavior and reducing code duplication.

1. **Using Extract Superclass**:
   - Select the class from which you want to extract a superclass.
   - Press Ctrl+Alt+Shift+T (Windows/Linux) or Cmd+Alt+Shift+T (macOS) and choose Extract Superclass.

- Select the methods and fields to be included in the new superclass and press Enter.

2. **Example**:
   - Suppose you have a class Employee with several methods and fields. You want to extract a superclass Person to promote common behavior. Select the class, press Ctrl+Alt+Shift+T, choose Extract Superclass, select the methods and fields to include, and press Enter. IntelliJ IDEA will create the superclass and update the class to extend it.

3. **Superclass Visibility**:
   - You can set the visibility (public, private, protected) of the new superclass in the extract superclass dialog.
   - This helps you control the scope of the new superclass.

4. **Extending Classes**:
   - IntelliJ IDEA automatically updates the class to extend the new superclass.
   - This ensures that the class inherits the behavior defined by the superclass.

Practical Examples

Let's explore practical examples of using refactoring tools in IntelliJ IDEA to improve code quality and maintainability.

Example 1: Renaming a Method

1. **Scenario**:
   - You have a method calculateTotal in a class and want to rename it to computeTotal.

2. **Steps**:
   - Select the method calculateTotal.
   - Press Shift+F6 to open the rename dialog.
   - Enter computeTotal and press Enter.
   - IntelliJ IDEA updates all references to this method throughout the codebase.

Example 2: Extracting a Method

1. **Scenario**:

- You have a block of code that calculates the discount in a method and want to extract it into a separate method.

2. **Steps**:
   - Select the block of code that calculates the discount.
   - Press Ctrl+Alt+M (Windows/Linux) or Cmd+Alt+M (macOS) to open the extract method dialog.
   - Enter calculateDiscount and press Enter.
   - IntelliJ IDEA creates a new method calculateDiscount and replaces the selected code with a call to this method.

Example 3: Moving a Class

1. **Scenario**:
   - You have a class Order in the package com.example.model and want to move it to com.example.entity.

2. **Steps**:
   - Select the class Order.
   - Press F6 to open the move dialog.
   - Choose the new package com.example.entity and press Enter.
   - IntelliJ IDEA moves the class and updates all references to it throughout the codebase.

Example 4: Extracting an Interface

1. **Scenario**:
   - You have a class PaymentService with several methods and want to extract an interface PaymentService to define the contract for this class.

2. **Steps**:
   - Select the class PaymentService.
   - Press Ctrl+Alt+Shift+T (Windows/Linux) or Cmd+Alt+Shift+T (macOS) and choose Extract Interface.
   - Select the methods to be included in the new interface and press Enter.
   - IntelliJ IDEA creates the interface and updates the class to implement it.

4.4 Using the Editor Efficiently

Efficiently using the editor in IntelliJ IDEA can significantly boost your productivity and streamline your coding workflow. This chapter delves into advanced editor features that help you write and edit code more effectively. We will explore multi-cursor editing, column selection mode, split editor, and distraction-free mode. By mastering these features, you can handle repetitive tasks with ease, manage large code files effectively, and maintain focus on your work.

Multi-Cursor Editing

Multi-cursor editing is a powerful feature in IntelliJ IDEA that allows you to place multiple cursors in the editor and make simultaneous changes. This feature is particularly useful for performing repetitive edits across multiple lines or making changes to similar code patterns.

Activating Multi-Cursor Editing

1. **Using the Mouse**:
   - Hold down the Alt key (Windows/Linux) or Option key (macOS).
   - Click at the locations where you want to place additional cursors.
2. **Using the Keyboard**:
   - Place the cursor at the starting location.
   - Press Ctrl+Alt+Shift+J (Windows/Linux) or Cmd+Ctrl+G (macOS) to select all occurrences of the current word.

Practical Uses of Multi-Cursor Editing

1. **Editing Multiple Lines**:
   - Multi-cursor editing is ideal for making changes to multiple lines at once. For example, you can add the same prefix or suffix to several lines, modify similar code structures, or update variable names across multiple lines.
2. **Inserting Text at Multiple Locations**:
   - You can insert the same text at multiple locations simultaneously. For instance, adding a method call or comment to multiple places in your code.
3. **Replacing Text**:

- o Use multi-cursor editing to replace instances of a text pattern. This can be more efficient than using find-and-replace in some cases, especially when you need to make contextual adjustments.

Example

Suppose you have the following lines of code and you want to add a prefix to all variable names:

```java
Copy code
int count = 10;
int total = 20;
int value = 30;
```

1. Place the cursor before count.
2. Hold Alt (Windows/Linux) or Option (macOS) and click before total and value to add multiple cursors.
3. Type the prefix, e.g., intVar_.

The modified code will be:

```java
Copy code
int intVar_count = 10;
int intVar_total = 20;
int intVar_value = 30;
```

Column Selection Mode

Column Selection Mode allows you to select and edit text in a rectangular area, which can be very handy for editing tabular data, aligning code, or working with columnar data structures.

Activating Column Selection Mode

1. **Using the Mouse**:
   - o Hold down the Alt key (Windows/Linux) or Option key (macOS).
   - o Drag the mouse to select the desired column.

2. **Using the Keyboard**:
    - o Place the cursor at the starting point.
    - o Press Shift+Alt+Insert (Windows/Linux) or Cmd+Shift+8 (macOS) to activate column selection mode.
    - o Use the arrow keys to expand the selection.

Practical Uses of Column Selection Mode

1. **Editing Columns of Text**:
    - o Column selection mode is perfect for editing columns of text, such as adding or removing text at specific columns across multiple lines.
2. **Aligning Code**:
    - o You can use column selection to align code elements, such as aligning variable declarations or method parameters for better readability.
3. **Working with Tabular Data**:
    - o This mode is useful for editing data in a tabular format, such as CSV files, by allowing you to select and edit specific columns directly.

Example

Suppose you have the following code and you want to align the variable names:

```java
Copy code
int count = 10;
int total  = 20;
int value   = 30;
```

1. Place the cursor at the beginning of the first line.
2. Press Shift+Alt+Insert (Windows/Linux) or Cmd+Shift+8 (macOS) to activate column selection mode.
3. Use the arrow keys to select the column range that includes the variable names.
4. Align the variable names by adjusting spaces as needed.

The modified code will be:

```java
Copy code
```

```
int count  = 10;
int total  = 20;
int value  = 30;
```

Split Editor

The Split Editor feature allows you to view and edit multiple files or different parts of the same file simultaneously. This is particularly useful for comparing code, referencing documentation, or working on multiple sections of a large file.

Activating Split Editor

1. **Vertical Split**:
   - Right-click the editor tab and select Split Vertically.
   - Alternatively, use the shortcut Ctrl+Alt+Shift+S (Windows/Linux) or Cmd+Option+Shift+S (macOS).
2. **Horizontal Split**:
   - Right-click the editor tab and select Split Horizontally.
   - Alternatively, use the shortcut Ctrl+Shift+Alt+S (Windows/Linux) or Cmd+Shift+Option+S (macOS).

Practical Uses of Split Editor

1. **Comparing Code**:
   - Use the split editor to compare code between two files or different sections of the same file side by side.
2. **Referencing Documentation**:
   - Open documentation or reference files in one pane while editing code in the other pane for easy access and better context.
3. **Editing Large Files**:
   - Split the editor to work on different sections of a large file simultaneously, reducing the need to scroll back and forth.

Example

Suppose you want to compare two methods in the same file:

1. Open the file in the editor.
2. Right-click the editor tab and select Split Vertically.
3. Scroll to the first method in the left pane and the second method in the right pane.

You can now view and compare both methods side by side.

Distraction-Free Mode

Distraction-Free Mode in IntelliJ IDEA helps you focus on your code by hiding all tool windows, menus, and other distractions. This mode provides a minimalist editing environment, ideal for deep work and concentration.

Activating Distraction-Free Mode

1. **Using the Menu**:
   o Go to View>Appearance>Enter Distraction-Free Mode.
2. **Using the Shortcut**:
   o Press Ctrl+Shift+F11 (Windows/Linux) or Cmd+Shift+F11 (macOS) to toggle distraction-free mode.

Practical Uses of Distraction-Free Mode

1. **Focusing on Code**:
   o Use distraction-free mode when you need to concentrate on writing or reviewing code without any interruptions.
2. **Reducing Eye Strain**:
   o The minimalist interface reduces visual clutter, which can help reduce eye strain during long coding sessions.
3. **Deep Work**:
   o Enter distraction-free mode for deep work sessions where you need to maintain high levels of focus and productivity.

Example

When you are working on a critical feature and need to minimize interruptions:

1. Press `Ctrl+Shift+F11` (Windows/Linux) or `Cmd+Shift+F11` (macOS) to enter distraction-free mode.
2. The editor will hide all tool windows, menus, and distractions, allowing you to focus solely on your code.
3. To exit distraction-free mode, press the same shortcut again.

Practical Workflow Integration

Integrating these editor features into your daily workflow can lead to significant improvements in productivity and code quality. Let's explore a practical scenario that demonstrates how to use multi-cursor editing, column selection mode, split editor, and distraction-free mode effectively.

Scenario: Refactoring a Legacy Codebase

1. **Analyzing and Understanding Code**:
   o Use the split editor to open the legacy code file in one pane and the refactored code in another pane.
   o Compare the old and new code side by side to understand the changes needed.
2. **Editing Multiple Lines Simultaneously**:
   o Use multi-cursor editing to update variable names or method calls across multiple lines.
   o For example, if a variable `oldVar` needs to be renamed to `newVar` in several places, use multi-cursor editing to place cursors at all occurrences and rename them simultaneously.
3. **Aligning Code for Readability**:
   o Use column selection mode to align variable declarations or method parameters.
   o Select the columns containing the variables or parameters and adjust the spacing to align them neatly.
4. **Focusing on Critical Sections**:
   o Enter distraction-free mode to work on critical sections of the code without any interruptions.
   o This helps you maintain focus and ensure the quality of your refactoring efforts.

4.5 Managing Code Style and Formatting

Maintaining a consistent code style and proper formatting is crucial for readability, maintainability, and collaboration in any software project. IntelliJ IDEA provides powerful tools to help you configure, manage, and enforce code style and formatting rules across your codebase. This chapter covers how to configure code style settings, reformat code, and use code inspections and quick fixes to ensure high-quality code.

Configuring Code Style Settings

IntelliJ IDEA allows you to configure code style settings to match your project's coding standards. These settings can be customized for various languages and applied consistently across your team.

Accessing Code Style Settings

1. **Opening the Settings Dialog**:
   - Navigate to File>Settings (Windows/Linux) or IntelliJ IDEA>Preferences (macOS).
   - In the Settings dialog, go to Editor>Code Style.
2. **Choosing a Language**:
   - Select the language you want to configure from the list on the left. IntelliJ IDEA supports configuring code styles for various languages, including Java, Kotlin, JavaScript, and more.

Configuring General Code Style Settings

1. **Tabs and Indents**:
   - Configure settings for tab and indent size, whether to use tabs or spaces, and continuation indent settings.
   - These settings ensure consistent indentation across your codebase.
2. **Spaces**:
   - Define when and where to use spaces in your code, such as around operators, after keywords, within parentheses, and more.
   - Consistent use of spaces improves code readability.
3. **Wrapping and Braces**:
   - Set rules for line wrapping, brace placement, and alignment.

o These settings help maintain a consistent code structure, especially for long lines of code or complex expressions.

4. **Blank Lines**:

   o Configure the number of blank lines before and after class declarations, methods, fields, and other code elements.

   o Proper use of blank lines helps to visually separate different sections of your code.

5. **JavaDoc**:

   o Customize JavaDoc formatting, including alignment, wrapping, and spacing.

   o Ensuring consistent documentation style enhances the readability and usability of your code documentation.

Saving and Sharing Code Style Settings

1. **Exporting Code Style Settings**:

   o You can export your code style settings to share with your team or apply to other projects.

   o In the Code Style settings window, click on the gear icon and choose Export to save the settings to a file.

2. **Importing Code Style Settings**:

   o To import code style settings, click on the gear icon in the Code Style settings window and choose Import to load settings from a file.

3. **Using EditorConfig**:

   o IntelliJ IDEA supports .editorconfig files, which provide a standard way to define and maintain consistent code styles across different editors and IDEs.

   o Create an .editorconfig file in your project root and define your code style rules. IntelliJ IDEA will automatically apply these settings.

Reformatting Code

IntelliJ IDEA makes it easy to reformat your code to conform to the configured code style settings. This ensures that your code remains clean and consistent, regardless of who wrote it.

Reformatting the Current File

1. **Using the Keyboard Shortcut**:
   o Press Ctrl+Alt+L (Windows/Linux) or Cmd+Option+L (macOS) to reformat the current file.
   o IntelliJ IDEA will apply the configured code style settings to the entire file.
2. **Using the Context Menu**:
   o Right-click in the editor and select Reformat Code from the context menu.
   o This option is also available in the Code menu.

Reformatting Multiple Files

1. **Using the Project View**:
   o In the Project view, select the files or directories you want to reformat.
   o Right-click and choose Reformat Code from the context menu.
2. **Using the Find Tool Window**:
   o Use the Find tool window to search for specific files or patterns.
   o Select the results and choose Reformat Code from the context menu.
3. **Using a Custom Scope**:
   o Create a custom scope to define a specific set of files or directories.
   o Navigate to File > Settings (Windows/Linux) or IntelliJ IDEA > Preferences (macOS), then go to Appearance & Behavior > Scopes.
   o Define your scope and apply it when reformatting code.

Reformatting Code Automatically

1. **Pre-Commit Hooks**:
   o Configure your version control system to run code reformatting as a pre-commit hook.
   o This ensures that all committed code adheres to the configured code style settings.
2. **File Watchers**:
   o Use file watchers to automatically reformat code when specific files are saved or modified.
   o Navigate to File > Settings (Windows/Linux) or IntelliJ IDEA > Preferences (macOS), then go to Tools > File Watchers.

o   Define a file watcher to trigger code reformatting on save.

Code Inspections and Quick Fixes

IntelliJ IDEA's code inspections analyze your code for potential issues and provide quick fixes to resolve them. These inspections help you maintain high code quality and adhere to best practices.

Configuring Code Inspections

1. **Accessing Inspection Settings**:
   o   Navigate to File>Settings (Windows/Linux) or IntelliJ IDEA>Preferences (macOS).
   o   Go to Editor>Inspections.
2. **Choosing Inspections**:
   o   Select the inspections you want to enable from the list on the left.
   o   Inspections are categorized by language and type, such as code style, performance, security, and more.
3. **Customizing Inspection Settings**:
   o   For each inspection, you can configure the severity level (e.g., warning, error) and customize its behavior.
   o   Use the search bar to quickly find specific inspections and configure their settings.

Running Code Inspections

1. **Running Inspections on the Current File**:
   o   Press Alt+Enter (Windows/Linux) or Option+Enter (macOS) to run inspections on the current file.
   o   IntelliJ IDEA will highlight potential issues and suggest quick fixes.
2. **Running Inspections on Multiple Files**:
   o   Navigate to Code>Inspect Code.
   o   Choose the scope (e.g., current file, whole project, custom scope) and run the inspections.
   o   The results will be displayed in the Inspection Results tool window.

Applying Quick Fixes

1. **Using the Quick Fix Popup**:
   - When IntelliJ IDEA detects an issue, it highlights the problematic code and shows a light bulb icon.
   - Press Alt+Enter (Windows/Linux) or Option+Enter (macOS) to open the quick fix popup.
   - Choose the appropriate quick fix from the list and press Enter to apply it.
2. **Batch Applying Quick Fixes**:
   - In the Inspection Results tool window, select the issues you want to fix.
   - Right-click and choose Apply Fix to apply the quick fixes to all selected issues.
3. **Example Quick Fixes**:
   - **Fixing Code Style Violations**: IntelliJ IDEA can automatically reformat code to match the configured style settings.
   - **Optimizing Imports**: Remove unused imports and organize the remaining imports according to your code style settings.
   - **Simplifying Expressions**: Replace complex expressions with simpler, equivalent ones to improve readability and performance.

Practical Workflow Integration

Integrating code style and formatting management into your daily workflow can lead to cleaner, more maintainable code. Let's explore a practical scenario that demonstrates how to configure code style settings, reformat code, and use code inspections and quick fixes effectively.

Scenario: Preparing Code for a Code Review

1. **Configuring Code Style Settings**:
   - Open the Code Style settings and configure the rules to match your project's coding standards.
   - Ensure that tabs, spaces, wrapping, and other settings are consistent with the project's guidelines.
2. **Reformatting Code**:
   - Before submitting code for review, reformat the code to ensure it adheres to the configured style settings.

- Use the Ctrl+Alt+L (Windows/Linux) or Cmd+Option+L (macOS) shortcut to reformat the current file.
- If you need to reformat multiple files, select them in the Project view and choose Reformat Code.

3. **Running Code Inspections**:
    - Run code inspections on the entire project to identify potential issues.
    - Navigate to Code>Inspect Code and choose the whole project scope.
    - Review the inspection results and apply quick fixes to resolve any detected issues.

4. **Applying Quick Fixes**:
    - Use the quick fix popup (Alt+Enter on Windows/Linux or Option+Enter on macOS) to address individual issues.
    - For batch fixing, use the Inspection Results tool window to select and fix multiple issues at once.

5. **Preparing for the Code Review**:
    - After reformatting and resolving inspection issues, review the code to ensure it is clean and follows best practices.
    - Submit the code for review with confidence, knowing that it adheres to the project's coding standards and is free of common issues.

Chapter 5: Debugging and Testing

Effective debugging and testing are critical for delivering high-quality software. IntelliJ IDEA offers a comprehensive set of tools to help you set up and manage debug configurations, use breakpoints and watches effectively, run and debug tests, utilize the test runner, and analyze code coverage. This chapter will guide you through these topics in detail, ensuring you have the knowledge to leverage IntelliJ IDEA's debugging and testing capabilities to their fullest.

5.1 Setting Up Debug Configurations

Debug configurations in IntelliJ IDEA allow you to specify how you want your application to run or debug. This includes setting parameters, specifying environments, and defining additional options for various run/debug scenarios.

Creating Run/Debug Configurations

Run/debug configurations are essential for specifying the conditions under which your application runs or gets debugged. These configurations can be tailored to different environments, modules, and parameters.

Creating a New Configuration

1. **Accessing the Run/Debug Configurations Dialog**:
   - Go to Run > Edit Configurations from the main menu.
   - Click the + button to add a new configuration.
2. **Selecting Configuration Type**:
   - Choose the appropriate configuration type based on your application or framework (e.g., Application, JUnit, TestNG, Maven, Gradle).
3. **Configuring Basic Settings**:
   - **Name**: Provide a meaningful name for your configuration.
   - **Main Class**: Specify the entry point for your application (for Java applications).
   - **Module**: Select the module to use.
4. **Setting Program Arguments and VM Options**:

- o **Program Arguments**: Specify any arguments to pass to your application.
- o **VM Options**: Configure Java Virtual Machine options, such as memory settings or system properties.

5. **Specifying Working Directory**:
   - o Define the working directory for the application.
6. **Environment Variables**:
   - o Set environment variables needed for your application.
7. **Before Launch**:
   - o Configure tasks to run before launching the application, such as building the project or running external tools.

Example Configuration: Java Application

Suppose you are setting up a run/debug configuration for a Java application with the main class com.example.Main.

1. Go to Run>Edit Configurations.
2. Click the + button and select Application.
3. Name the configuration Run MyApp.
4. Set the Main Class to com.example.Main.
5. Choose the module that contains the main class.
6. Optionally, add any program arguments or VM options.
7. Click OK to save the configuration.

Attaching to Remote Processes

IntelliJ IDEA allows you to attach the debugger to a remote process running on a different machine or environment. This is useful for debugging applications running in production or on remote servers.

Setting Up Remote Debugging

1. **Enable Remote Debugging on the Target Application**:
   - o Modify the startup script or command to include remote debugging options.
   - o Example for a Java application:

```sh
Copy code
java -agentlib:jdwp=transport=dt_socket,server=y,suspend=n,address=*:5005 -jar
myapp.jar
```

- o This command opens a debug port on 5005.
2. **Creating a Remote Debug Configuration in IntelliJ IDEA**:
    - o Go to Run > Edit Configurations.
    - o Click the + button and select Remote.
    - o Name the configuration Remote Debug MyApp.
    - o Set the Host to the remote machine's IP address.
    - o Set the Port to 5005 (or the port you configured).
3. **Attaching the Debugger**:
    - o Start the remote application with the debug options.
    - o In IntelliJ IDEA, select the Remote Debug MyApp configuration and click the Debug button.
    - o IntelliJ IDEA will connect to the remote process, allowing you to debug it as if it were running locally.

Debugging Multi-Module Projects

Multi-module projects in IntelliJ IDEA involve multiple modules, each potentially representing a different part of the application or a different library. Setting up debugging for such projects requires configuring the appropriate modules and their dependencies.

Configuring Multi-Module Debugging

1. **Ensure Module Dependencies are Set Correctly**:
    - o Open the Project Structure dialog (File > Project Structure).
    - o Go to Modules and verify that dependencies between modules are correctly defined.
2. **Creating a Composite Debug Configuration**:
    - o Go to Run > Edit Configurations.
    - o Click the + button and select Compound.
    - o Name the configuration Debug Multi-Module.

- Click Add Configuration and include the run/debug configurations for each module you want to debug.
3. **Running the Composite Configuration**:
   - Select the Debug Multi-Module configuration and click the Debug button.
   - IntelliJ IDEA will start debugging all specified modules concurrently, allowing you to set breakpoints and step through code across modules.

Example: Debugging a Web Application with Backend and Frontend Modules

Suppose you have a multi-module project with backend and frontend modules.

1. **Create Debug Configurations for Each Module**:
   - For the backend module:
     - Go to Run > Edit Configurations.
     - Click + and select Application.
     - Name it Debug Backend.
     - Set the main class to com.example.backend.Main.
   - For the frontend module:
     - Click + and select Application.
     - Name it Debug Frontend.
     - Set the main class to com.example.frontend.Main.
2. **Create a Composite Configuration**:
   - Go to Run > Edit Configurations.
   - Click + and select Compound.
   - Name it Debug Full Stack.
   - Add Debug Backend and Debug Frontend to the composite configuration.
3. **Debugging**:
   - Select Debug Full Stack and click the Debug button.
   - Set breakpoints in both backend and frontend modules.
   - IntelliJ IDEA will start both modules, allowing you to debug the interaction between them.

5.2 Using Breakpoints and Watches

Breakpoints and watches are essential tools in any debugger, allowing you to pause execution, inspect variables, and evaluate expressions at specific points in your code.

Setting and Managing Breakpoints

Breakpoints enable you to pause the execution of your application at specific lines of code or conditions. IntelliJ IDEA provides various types of breakpoints to suit different debugging needs.

Types of Breakpoints

1. **Line Breakpoints**:
   - Standard breakpoints set on a specific line of code.
   - Execution pauses when the line is reached.
2. **Method Breakpoints**:
   - Set on a method to pause execution when the method is entered or exited.
3. **Field Breakpoints**:
   - Pause execution when a specific field is accessed or modified.
4. **Exception Breakpoints**:
   - Pause execution when a specific exception is thrown.
5. **Conditional Breakpoints**:
   - Standard breakpoints with a condition that must be met for the breakpoint to trigger.

Setting Breakpoints

1. **Line Breakpoints**:
   - Click the gutter (left margin) next to the line number where you want to set the breakpoint.
   - A red dot indicates the breakpoint.
2. **Method Breakpoints**:
   - Right-click the method signature in the editor.
   - Select Toggle Method Breakpoint.
3. **Field Breakpoints**:
   - Right-click the field in the editor.
   - Select Toggle Field Breakpoint.
4. **Exception Breakpoints**:
   - Go to Run>View Breakpoints (Ctrl+Shift+F8).

- o Click + and select Java Exception Breakpoint.
- o Choose the exception class to break on.

Conditional Breakpoints

Conditional breakpoints allow you to pause execution only when certain conditions are met, making them invaluable for complex debugging scenarios.

Setting a Conditional Breakpoint

1. **Add a Condition to an Existing Breakpoint**:
   - o Right-click an existing breakpoint (red dot) in the gutter.
   - o Select More (or press Ctrl+Shift+F8).
2. **Specify the Condition**:
   - o In the Breakpoint dialog, check the Condition box.
   - o Enter a boolean expression that evaluates to true when you want the breakpoint to trigger.
   - o For example, counter > 100.
3. **Advanced Options**:
   - o You can also set actions to be performed when the breakpoint is hit, such as logging a message or running a script.

Watches and Evaluate Expressions

Watches and the Evaluate Expressions feature in IntelliJ IDEA allow you to inspect and manipulate variables and expressions during debugging.

Adding Watches

1. **Setting a Watch**:
   - o During a debug session, select a variable or expression in the editor.
   - o Right-click and choose Add to Watches.
2. **Managing Watches**:
   - o Watches appear in the Variables pane of the Debug tool window.
   - o You can add, remove, or modify watches as needed.

Evaluating Expressions

1. **Using the Evaluate Expression Dialog**:
   - During a debug session, press Alt+F8 (Windows/Linux) or Option+F8 (macOS).
   - The Evaluate Expression dialog appears.
2. **Entering and Evaluating Expressions**:
   - Enter any valid expression or variable name in the dialog.
   - Click Evaluate to see the result.
3. **Modifying Variables**:
   - You can modify the values of variables within the Evaluate Expression dialog by assigning new values.
   - Example: counter = 50.

Practical Example: Debugging a Loop

Suppose you are debugging a loop that calculates the sum of an array, and you suspect there's an issue when the array length is greater than 10.

1. **Setting a Breakpoint in the Loop**:
   - Set a line breakpoint inside the loop.
2. **Adding a Conditional Breakpoint**:
   - Right-click the breakpoint and select More.
   - Add the condition array.length> 10.
3. **Adding a Watch**:
   - Select the sum variable and add it to watches.
4. **Running the Debugger**:
   - Start the debug session.
   - Execution will pause when the condition array.length> 10 is met.
   - Inspect the sum variable in the Watches pane to analyze the issue.

5.3 Running and Debugging Tests

IntelliJ IDEA supports various testing frameworks, making it easy to run and debug tests directly from the IDE. This section covers supported testing frameworks, creating and running tests, and debugging tests.

Supported Testing Frameworks

IntelliJ IDEA supports multiple testing frameworks, including JUnit and TestNG for Java applications.

JUnit

JUnit is a widely-used testing framework for Java. IntelliJ IDEA fully integrates with JUnit, allowing you to create, run, and debug JUnit tests easily.

1. **Creating a JUnit Test**:
     o Right-click the class you want to test.
     o Select New>JUnit Test.
2. **Running JUnit Tests**:
     o Right-click the test class or method and select Run.
     o Alternatively, use the run/debug configuration for more advanced options.
3. **Debugging JUnit Tests**:
     o Right-click the test class or method and select Debug.

TestNG

TestNG is another popular testing framework for Java, offering advanced features like parallel test execution and data-driven testing.

1. **Creating a TestNG Test**:
     o Right-click the class you want to test.
     o Select New>TestNG Class.
2. **Running TestNG Tests**:
     o Right-click the test class or method and select Run.
     o Use the run/debug configuration for more options.
3. **Debugging TestNG Tests**:
     o Right-click the test class or method and select Debug.

Creating and Running Tests

Creating and running tests in IntelliJ IDEA is straightforward, thanks to the built-in support for popular testing frameworks.

Example: Creating and Running JUnit Tests

1. **Creating a Test Class**:
   - ○ Right-click the class or package you want to test.
   - ○ Select New>JUnit Test Class.
   - ○ Choose the methods you want to test and click OK.
2. **Writing Test Methods**:
   - ○ Annotate your test methods with @Test.
   - ○ Example:

```java
Copy code
import org.junit.Test;
import static org.junit.Assert.*;

public class MyTests {
    @Test
    public void testAddition() {
        int sum = 1 + 1;
assertEquals(2, sum);
    }
}
```

3. **Running Tests**:
   - ○ Right-click the test class or individual test method.
   - ○ Select Run to execute the tests.

Example: Creating and Running TestNG Tests

1. **Creating a TestNG Class**:
   - ○ Right-click the class or package you want to test.
   - ○ Select New>TestNG Class.
2. **Writing Test Methods**:
   - ○ Annotate your test methods with @Test.
   - ○ Example:

```java
Copy code
import org.testng.annotations.Test;
import static org.testng.Assert.*;
```

```
public class MyTests {
    @Test
    public void testAddition() {
        int sum = 1 + 1;
assertEquals(2, sum);
    }
}
```

3. **Running Tests**:
    - o Right-click the test class or individual test method.
    - o Select Run to execute the tests.

Debugging Tests

Debugging tests in IntelliJ IDEA involves setting breakpoints within your test methods or the code being tested.

Steps to Debug Tests

1. **Set Breakpoints**:
    - o Open the test class or the class being tested.
    - o Click the gutter next to the line number to set breakpoints.
2. **Debugging a Test**:
    - o Right-click the test class or method.
    - o Select Debug.
3. **Inspecting Variables and Evaluating Expressions**:
    - o Use the Debug tool window to inspect variables, watches, and evaluate expressions.
4. **Stepping Through Code**:
    - o Use the step over, step into, and step out buttons to navigate through your code.

Practical Example: Debugging a TestNG Test

Suppose you have a TestNG test for a calculator application and want to debug the add method.

1. **Set a Breakpoint in the add Method**:

- o Open the Calculator class and set a breakpoint in the add method.
- o Example:

```java
Copy code
public class Calculator {
    public int add(int a, int b) {
        // Set a breakpoint here
        return a + b;
    }
}
```

2. **Debug the Test**:
   - o Open the CalculatorTest class.
   - o Right-click the test method testAddition and select Debug.
3. **Inspect Variables**:
   - o When execution pauses at the breakpoint, inspect the values of a and b.
4. **Step Through Code**:
   - o Use the debugger to step through the add method and verify its behavior.

5.4 Utilizing the Test Runner

The Test Runner in IntelliJ IDEA provides a powerful interface for running and managing tests. It displays test results, allows rerunning failed tests, and provides insights into test performance.

Test Runner UI

The Test Runner UI displays the status of your tests, including passed, failed, and ignored tests. It provides a clear and organized view of test results.

Key Components of the Test Runner UI

1. **Test Tree**:
   - o Displays the hierarchy of tests and their statuses.
   - o Tests are grouped by packages, classes, and methods.
2. **Test Progress**:
   - o Shows the progress of test execution with a visual progress bar.

- o Indicates the number of tests passed, failed, and ignored.
3. **Test Results**:
     - o Provides detailed information about each test, including the execution time and any associated messages or stack traces.
4. **Toolbar**:
     - o Contains buttons for running, rerunning, and stopping tests.
     - o Provides options to export test results, filter tests, and view output.

Analyzing Test Results

The Test Runner UI provides detailed information about test results, allowing you to analyze and understand test outcomes.

Viewing Test Results

1. **Select a Test**:
     - o Click on a test in the test tree to view its details.
     - o The right pane displays the test output, including logs and stack traces for failed tests.
2. **Navigating to Source**:
     - o Double-click a test method in the test tree to navigate to its source code.
     - o This helps you quickly locate and address issues in your code.
3. **Filtering Tests**:
     - o Use the filter options in the toolbar to focus on specific test outcomes (e.g., failed tests, ignored tests).

Practical Example: Analyzing a Failed Test

Suppose a test method testAddition in the CalculatorTest class fails.

1. **View the Failed Test**:
     - o Open the Test Runner tool window.
     - o Click on testAddition in the test tree.
2. **Analyze the Failure**:
     - o The right pane displays the stack trace and any assertion messages.
     - o Identify the cause of the failure by examining the stack trace.

3. **Navigate to the Source**:
   - Double-click testAddition in the test tree to open its source code.
   - Review the test method and the code being tested to identify and fix the issue.

Rerunning Failed Tests

IntelliJ IDEA allows you to rerun failed tests, making it easy to verify fixes and ensure all tests pass.

Rerunning Failed Tests

1. **Using the Test Runner UI**:
   - In the Test Runner tool window, click the Rerun Failed Tests button in the toolbar.
   - IntelliJ IDEA will rerun only the tests that failed.
2. **Rerunning from the Context Menu**:
   - Right-click a failed test method in the test tree.
   - Select Run 'testMethod' to rerun the specific test.
3. **Automated Reruns**:
   - Configure IntelliJ IDEA to automatically rerun failed tests after a code change.
   - Go to File > Settings (Windows/Linux) or IntelliJ IDEA > Preferences (macOS), then Build, Execution, Deployment > Compiler.
   - Enable Automatically rebuild project on changes and Rerun failed tests automatically.

Practical Example: Rerunning a Failed Test

Suppose the testAddition method failed, and you have fixed the issue in the Calculator class.

1. **Rerun the Failed Test**:
   - Open the Test Runner tool window.
   - Click the Rerun Failed Tests button.
2. **Verify the Fix**:
   - IntelliJ IDEA reruns the failed tests.
   - Ensure that testAddition passes, indicating the issue is resolved.

5.5 Analyzing Code Coverage

Code coverage analysis helps you understand how much of your code is being tested. IntelliJ IDEA provides tools to measure and visualize code coverage.

Configuring Code Coverage

Configuring code coverage in IntelliJ IDEA involves setting up the necessary plugins and specifying the coverage options.

Enabling Code Coverage

1. **Install the Coverage Plugin** (if not already installed):
   - Go to File > Settings (Windows/Linux) or IntelliJ IDEA > Preferences (macOS).
   - Navigate to Plugins and search for the Coverage plugin.
   - Install and restart IntelliJ IDEA if required.
2. **Configuring Coverage Settings**:
   - Go to Run > Edit Configurations.
   - Select a run/debug configuration.
   - In the Configuration tab, click Modify options and select Coverage.

Running with Coverage

Running tests with code coverage provides insights into which parts of your code are being exercised by your tests.

Running Tests with Coverage

1. **Run with Coverage**:
   - Right-click the test class or method.
   - Select Run 'Tests' with Coverage.
2. **View Coverage Results**:
   - The Coverage tool window opens, displaying the coverage summary.
   - Coverage results are also shown in the editor, with different colors indicating covered, partially covered, and uncovered lines.

Interpreting Coverage Results

IntelliJ IDEA provides detailed coverage reports, helping you identify areas of your code that need more testing.

Coverage Tool Window

1. **Summary View**:
   - Displays the overall coverage percentage for classes, methods, and lines.
   - Provides a quick overview of test coverage.
2. **Detailed View**:
   - Lists packages, classes, and methods with their respective coverage percentages.
   - Allows you to drill down into specific parts of your code.

Editor Annotations

1. **Color Annotations**:
   - Green: Fully covered lines.
   - Yellow: Partially covered lines.
   - Red: Uncovered lines.
2. **Navigating Coverage Data**:
   - Click on the colored markers in the gutter to navigate to the corresponding lines in your code.
   - Review the coverage annotations to identify and address gaps in your tests.

Practical Example: Analyzing Code Coverage

Suppose you want to analyze the coverage of your Calculator class tests.

1. **Run Tests with Coverage**:
   - Right-click the CalculatorTest class.
   - Select Run 'CalculatorTest' with Coverage.
2. **View Coverage Summary**:
   - Open the Coverage tool window to see the overall coverage percentage.
3. **Inspect Coverage in the Editor**:

- o   Open the Calculator class.
- o   Review the color annotations to identify uncovered or partially covered lines.

4. **Improve Test Coverage**:
   - o   Write additional tests to cover uncovered lines.
   - o   Rerun tests with coverage to verify improvements.

Chapter 6: Building and Running Applications

In this chapter, we delve into the processes and tools necessary for building, running, packaging, deploying, and integrating applications within IntelliJ IDEA. Mastering these concepts will enable you to streamline your development workflow, ensure consistent builds, and facilitate automated testing and deployment.

6.1 Configuring Build Tools (Maven, Gradle)

Build tools are essential for managing project dependencies, compiling source code, and packaging applications. IntelliJ IDEA provides excellent support for popular build tools like Maven and Gradle.

Setting Up Maven Projects

Maven is a widely-used build automation tool that follows a convention-over-configuration approach. It simplifies the build process by managing project dependencies and lifecycle.

Creating a Maven Project

1. **Starting a New Project**:
   - Open IntelliJ IDEA and select New Project from the Welcome screen.
   - Choose Maven from the list of project types.
2. **Configuring Project Details**:
   - Specify the project's group ID, artifact ID, and version.
   - Choose the project's location on your file system.
   - Select a Java SDK to use for the project.
3. **Setting Up the Project Structure**:
   - IntelliJ IDEA will generate a standard Maven project structure with directories like src/main/java, src/test/java, src/main/resources, and src/test/resources.

Configuring the pom.xml

The pom.xml (Project Object Model) file is the core of a Maven project, defining project dependencies, plugins, and build configurations.

1. **Adding Dependencies**:
   - Open pom.xml and locate the <dependencies> section.
   - Add dependencies using the following syntax:

   ```xml
   Copy code
   <dependency>
   <groupId>org.springframework.boot</groupId>
   <artifactId>spring-boot-starter-web</artifactId>
   <version>2.5.4</version>
   </dependency>
   ```

2. **Configuring Plugins**:
   - Plugins enhance the build process with additional tasks like compiling code, packaging artifacts, and running tests.
   - Example of configuring the Maven Compiler Plugin:

   ```xml
   Copy code
   <build>
   <plugins>
   <plugin>
   <groupId>org.apache.maven.plugins</groupId>
   <artifactId>maven-compiler-plugin</artifactId>
   <version>3.8.1</version>
   <configuration>
   <source>1.8</source>
   <target>1.8</target>
   </configuration>
   </plugin>
   </plugins>
   </build>
   ```

Configuring Gradle Builds

Gradle is a versatile build automation tool that supports both declarative and imperative build configurations. It uses a Groovy or Kotlin DSL for defining project settings.

Creating a Gradle Project

1. **Starting a New Project**:
   - Open IntelliJ IDEA and select New Project.
   - Choose Gradle from the list of project types.
2. **Configuring Project Details**:
   - Specify the project's group ID, artifact ID, and version.
   - Choose the project's location on your file system.
   - Select a Java SDK to use for the project.
3. **Setting Up the Project Structure**:
   - IntelliJ IDEA will generate a standard Gradle project structure with directories like src/main/java, src/test/java, src/main/resources, and src/test/resources.

Configuring the build.gradle

The build.gradle file is the primary configuration file for a Gradle project, defining dependencies, plugins, and build tasks.

1. **Adding Dependencies**:
   - Open build.gradle and locate the dependencies section.
   - Add dependencies using the following syntax:

   ```groovy
   Copy code
   dependencies {
       implementation 'org.springframework.boot:spring-boot-starter-web:2.5.4'
   }
   ```

2. **Configuring Plugins**:
   - Plugins extend Gradle's functionality with additional tasks and configurations.
   - Example of applying the Java plugin and configuring the Java version:

   ```groovy
   ```

```
Copy code
plugins {
  id 'java'
}

java {
sourceCompatibility = JavaVersion.VERSION_1_8
targetCompatibility = JavaVersion.VERSION_1_8
}
```

Managing Dependencies

Managing dependencies is a critical aspect of using build tools. Both Maven and Gradle provide mechanisms to handle dependencies efficiently.

Maven Dependency Management

1. **Scopes**:
   - Maven supports different dependency scopes like compile, test, provided, and runtime to control the classpath during various build phases.
2. **Transitive Dependencies**:
   - Maven resolves transitive dependencies automatically. If a dependency relies on other libraries, Maven includes those in the classpath.
3. **Exclusions**:
   - You can exclude specific transitive dependencies if they are not needed.

   ```xml
   Copy code
   <dependency>
   <groupId>com.example</groupId>
   <artifactId>example-lib</artifactId>
   <version>1.0.0</version>
   <exclusions>
   <exclusion>
   <groupId>org.unwanted</groupId>
   <artifactId>unwanted-lib</artifactId>
   </exclusion>
   </exclusions>
   </dependency>
   ```

Gradle Dependency Management

1. **Configurations**:
   - o Gradle uses configurations like implementation, testImplementation, and runtimeOnly to manage dependencies.
2. **Transitive Dependencies**:
   - o Gradle resolves transitive dependencies by default but allows fine-grained control over them.
3. **Exclusions**:
   - o You can exclude specific dependencies using the exclude method.

```groovy
Copy code
dependencies {
    implementation('com.example:example-lib:1.0.0') {
        exclude group: 'org.unwanted', module: 'unwanted-lib'
    }
}
```

6.2 Running Applications

Running applications from within IntelliJ IDEA involves configuring run/debug configurations, running from the IDE, and integrating external tools.

Running from the IDE

IntelliJ IDEA provides a straightforward way to run and debug applications directly from the IDE.

Running a Java Application

1. **Using the Run Menu**:
   - o Open the class with the main method.
   - o Click the green Run button in the toolbar or press Shift + F10.
2. **Context Menu**:
   - o Right-click the class with the main method.
   - o Select Run 'ClassName.main()'.

Configuring Run/Debug Configurations

Run/debug configurations define how to run and debug your applications.

Creating a Run Configuration

1. **Open the Run/Debug Configurations Dialog**:
   - Go to Run > Edit Configurations.
2. **Add a New Configuration**:
   - Click the + button and select the configuration type (e.g., Application for Java applications).
3. **Configure the Main Settings**:
   - Specify the main class, program arguments, and working directory.
   - Example:
     - Main class: com.example.Main
     - Program arguments: --server.port=8080
     - Working directory: /path/to/project

Creating a Debug Configuration

Debug configurations are similar to run configurations but are used to start applications in debug mode.

1. **Enable Debug Options**:
   - Follow the steps to create a run configuration.
   - Click Modify options and select Debug options if necessary.
2. **Setting Breakpoints**:
   - Open the source code and click the gutter next to the line number to set breakpoints.
3. **Starting the Debugger**:
   - Select the debug configuration and click the green bug icon in the toolbar or press Shift + F9.

Running External Tools

IntelliJ IDEA allows you to integrate and run external tools as part of your development workflow.

Configuring External Tools

1. **Open External Tools Settings**:
   - ○ Go to File > Settings (Windows/Linux) or IntelliJ IDEA > Preferences (macOS).
   - ○ Navigate to Tools > External Tools.
2. **Add a New Tool**:
   - ○ Click Add and fill in the necessary details.
   - ○ Specify the name, group, and executable path.
   - ○ Example:
     - ▪ Name: MyTool
     - ▪ Group: Custom Tools
     - ▪ Program: /path/to/tool
3. **Running the Tool**:
   - ○ Right-click in the editor or project view and select External Tools > MyTool.

6.3 Packaging and Deploying Applications

Packaging and deploying applications involves creating artifacts, using build tools for packaging, and deploying to application servers.

Creating Artifacts

Artifacts are the packaged versions of your application, such as JAR, WAR, or EAR files.

Configuring Artifacts

1. **Open the Project Structure Dialog**:
   - ○ Go to File > Project Structure.
2. **Add a New Artifact**:
   - ○ Navigate to Artifacts and click + to add a new artifact.
   - ○ Select the artifact type (e.g., JAR, WAR).
3. **Configure Artifact Settings**:
   - ○ Specify the output directory, include/exclude files, and configure the build process.
   - ○ Example for a JAR artifact:
     - ▪ Output directory: /path/to/output

- Include compiled classes and resources.

Packaging with Maven/Gradle

Build tools like Maven and Gradle can automate the packaging process.

Packaging with Maven

1. **Configure the pom.xml**:
   - Ensure you have the necessary plugins configured.
   - Example for a JAR artifact:

   ```xml
   Copy code
   <build>
   <plugins>
   <plugin>
   <groupId>org.apache.maven.plugins</groupId>
   <artifactId>maven-jar-plugin</artifactId>
   <version>3.2.0</version>
   </plugin>
   </plugins>
   </build>
   ```

2. **Run the Package Goal**:
   - Open the terminal and run the following command:

   ```sh
   Copy code
   mvn clean package
   ```

Packaging with Gradle

1. **Configure the build.gradle**:
   - Ensure you have the necessary plugins and tasks configured.
   - Example for a JAR artifact:

   ```groovy
   Copy code
   plugins {
   ```

```
    id 'java'
}

jar {
archiveBaseName = 'myapp'
archiveVersion = '1.0.0'
destinationDirectory = file("$buildDir/libs")
}
```

2. **Run the Build Task**:
   - Open the terminal and run the following command:

```sh
Copy code
gradle clean build
```

Deploying to Application Servers

IntelliJ IDEA supports deploying applications to various application servers, including Tomcat, Jetty, and JBoss.

Configuring Deployment

1. **Open the Run/Debug Configurations Dialog**:
   - Go to Run > Edit Configurations.
2. **Add a New Configuration**:
   - Click the + button and select the server type (e.g., Tomcat Server).
3. **Configure Deployment Settings**:
   - Specify the server settings, deployment artifacts, and startup parameters.
   - Example for Tomcat:
     - Tomcat Home: /path/to/tomcat
     - Deployment: Select the WAR artifact to deploy.
4. **Starting the Server**:
   - Select the server configuration and click the green run button or press Shift + F10.

6.4 Working with Continuous Integration

Continuous integration (CI) involves automatically building and testing your code each time changes are pushed to the repository. Integrating IntelliJ IDEA with CI tools streamlines the development workflow and ensures consistent quality.

Integrating with CI/CD Tools

CI/CD tools like Jenkins, GitLab CI, and Travis CI can be integrated with IntelliJ IDEA to automate the build and deployment process.

Setting Up Jenkins Integration

1. **Install Jenkins**:
   - Download and install Jenkins from the official website.
   - Configure Jenkins with the necessary plugins (e.g., Git, Maven, Gradle).
2. **Create a Jenkins Job**:
   - Open Jenkins and create a new job (e.g., Freestyle Project).
   - Configure the source code repository (e.g., Git).
   - Set up build triggers (e.g., GitHub webhook).
3. **Configure the Build Step**:
   - Add a build step to invoke Maven or Gradle.
   - Example for Maven:

     ```sh
     Copy code
     mvn clean package
     ```

4. **Integrate IntelliJ IDEA**:
   - Use the Jenkins plugin for IntelliJ IDEA to view build statuses and logs directly from the IDE.

Setting Up GitLab CI

1. **Create a .gitlab-ci.yml File**:
   - Define the CI/CD pipeline in the .gitlab-ci.yml file.
   - Example for a Maven project:

     ```yaml
     Copy code
     ```

```
stages:
  - build

build_job:
  stage: build
  script:
    - mvn clean package
```

2. **Push to GitLab**:
   - o Commit and push the .gitlab-ci.yml file to your GitLab repository.
3. **View Pipeline Status**:
   - o Check the CI/CD pipeline status on GitLab to ensure the build process is successful.

Setting Up Build Pipelines

Build pipelines automate the process of building, testing, and deploying your code.

Configuring a Jenkins Pipeline

1. **Create a Jenkins Pipeline Job**:
   - o Open Jenkins and create a new pipeline job.
2. **Define the Pipeline Script**:
   - o Write the pipeline script using Jenkins Pipeline DSL (Groovy).
   - o Example:

```groovy
Copy code
pipeline {
    agent any
    stages {
        stage('Build') {
            steps {
                sh 'mvn clean package'
            }
        }
        stage('Test') {
            steps {
                sh 'mvn test'
            }
```

```
        }
        stage('Deploy') {
            steps {
sh 'mvn deploy'
            }
        }
    }
}
```

3. **Run the Pipeline**:
   o Trigger the pipeline manually or set up automatic triggers (e.g., on code push).

Configuring a GitLab CI Pipeline

1. **Define the Pipeline in .gitlab-ci.yml**:
   o Write the pipeline stages and jobs.
   o Example:

   ```yaml
   yaml
   Copy code
   stages:
     - build
     - test
     - deploy

   build_job:
     stage: build
     script:
       - mvn clean package

   test_job:
     stage: test
     script:
       - mvn test

   deploy_job:
     stage: deploy
     script:
       - mvn deploy
   ```

2. **Commit and Push**:
   - o Commit the .gitlab-ci.yml file and push it to the repository.
3. **Monitor Pipeline**:
   - o Monitor the pipeline progress and results on GitLab.

Automated Testing and Deployment

Automated testing and deployment are crucial for maintaining code quality and ensuring reliable releases.

Automated Testing

1. **Unit Tests**:
   - o Write unit tests using frameworks like JUnit or TestNG.
   - o Integrate unit tests into the build process.
2. **Integration Tests**:
   - o Write integration tests to verify the interactions between different parts of your application.
   - o Configure the build tool to run integration tests.
3. **Continuous Testing**:
   - o Set up CI tools to run tests automatically on code changes.
   - o Use test coverage tools to measure the extent of your tests.

Automated Deployment

1. **Deployment Scripts**:
   - o Write deployment scripts to automate the deployment process.
   - o Example using a shell script:

   ```sh
   Copy code
   #!/bin/bash
   scp target/myapp.waruser@server:/path/to/deploy
   ssh user@server 'bash /path/to/restart-server.sh'
   ```

2. **Integrate with CI/CD**:
   - o Configure your CI/CD tool to run deployment scripts after successful builds.

- o   Ensure proper environment configurations and access controls.
3. **Monitoring and Rollbacks**:
     - o   Set up monitoring tools to track application performance after deployment.
     - o   Implement rollback mechanisms to revert to a previous stable version in case of issues.

By understanding and utilizing IntelliJ IDEA's capabilities for building and running applications, you can significantly enhance your development workflow. From configuring build tools and running applications to packaging, deploying, and integrating with CI/CD tools, this chapter provides comprehensive insights and practical steps to streamline your software development process.

Chapter 7: Advanced Features and Plugins

IntelliJ IDEA is renowned for its extensive feature set and robust plugin ecosystem. In this chapter, we'll explore advanced features and plugins that can enhance your development experience. We'll cover how to install and manage plugins, integrate third-party tools, utilize the database tools, customize keymaps and macros, and leverage live templates.

7.1 IntelliJ IDEA Plugins

Plugins are a powerful way to extend the functionality of IntelliJ IDEA, providing additional tools and integrations that can significantly enhance your productivity.

Plugin Repository Overview

IntelliJ IDEA's plugin repository is a comprehensive collection of plugins developed by both JetBrains and third-party developers. These plugins cover a wide range of functionalities, from language support and version control integrations to user interface enhancements and productivity tools.

Accessing the Plugin Repository

To access the plugin repository:

1. **Open the Settings/Preferences Dialog**:
   o Go to File>Settings (Windows/Linux) or IntelliJ IDEA>Preferences (macOS).
2. **Navigate to the Plugins Section**:
   o Select Plugins from the left-hand menu.
3. **Browse and Search for Plugins**:
   o Use the Marketplace tab to browse popular and recommended plugins.
   o Use the search bar to find specific plugins by name or keyword.

Installing and Managing Plugins

Installing and managing plugins is straightforward, allowing you to customize IntelliJ IDEA to suit your development needs.

Installing Plugins

1. **From the Plugin Repository**:
   - o   Find the desired plugin in the Marketplace tab.
   - o   Click Install to download and install the plugin.
   - o   Restart IntelliJ IDEA if prompted.
2. **From a Local File**:
   - o   If you have a plugin file (.zip or .jar), click the gear icon in the Plugins section.
   - o   Select Install Plugin from Disk....
   - o   Navigate to the plugin file and click Open.

Managing Plugins

1. **Enable or Disable Plugins**:
   - o   Go to the Installed tab in the Plugins section.
   - o   Use the checkbox next to each plugin to enable or disable it.
2. **Update Plugins**:
   - o   IntelliJ IDEA automatically checks for updates to installed plugins.
   - o   To manually check for updates, click the Update button if an update is available.
3. **Uninstall Plugins**:
   - o   In the Installed tab, click the Uninstall button next to the plugin you want to remove.

Recommended Plugins for Developers

Here are some essential plugins that can enhance your development workflow:

1. **Lombok**:
   - o   Simplifies Java development by generating boilerplate code for getters, setters, constructors, etc.
2. **CheckStyle-IDEA**:
   - o   Integrates CheckStyle into IntelliJ IDEA for code style checking.

3. **SonarLint**:
   - Provides real-time feedback on code quality and detects bugs and security vulnerabilities.
4. **Docker**:
   - Integrates Docker support, allowing you to manage containers and images directly from the IDE.
5. **Kubernetes**:
   - Provides Kubernetes support for managing clusters and deployments within IntelliJ IDEA.
6. **Markdown Support**:
   - Adds support for editing and previewing Markdown files.
7. **.ignore**:
   - Helps manage .gitignore and other ignore files with syntax highlighting and templates.

7.2 Integrating Third-Party Tools

IntelliJ IDEA can be integrated with a variety of third-party tools, enhancing its capabilities and providing a seamless development experience.

Integrating with Docker

Docker is a platform for developing, shipping, and running applications in containers. IntelliJ IDEA's Docker plugin allows you to manage Docker containers, images, and networks directly from the IDE.

Setting Up Docker Integration

1. **Install the Docker Plugin**:
   - Go to the Plugins section in the settings and install the Docker plugin.
2. **Configure Docker**:
   - Go to File > Settings (Windows/Linux) or IntelliJ IDEA > Preferences (macOS).
   - Navigate to Build, Execution, Deployment > Docker.
   - Click the + button to add a Docker configuration.
   - Specify the Docker API endpoint (e.g., unix:///var/run/docker.sock for Linux/macOS or tcp://localhost:2375 for Windows).

3. **Using Docker in IntelliJ IDEA**:
   - Open the Docker tool window (View>Tool Windows>Docker).
   - Manage Docker containers, images, and networks directly from the IDE.

Using Kubernetes with IntelliJ IDEA

Kubernetes is an open-source platform for automating the deployment, scaling, and management of containerized applications. IntelliJ IDEA supports Kubernetes through its Kubernetes plugin.

Setting Up Kubernetes Integration

1. **Install the Kubernetes Plugin**:
   - Go to the Plugins section in the settings and install the Kubernetes plugin.
2. **Configure Kubernetes**:
   - Go to File>Settings (Windows/Linux) or IntelliJ IDEA>Preferences (macOS).
   - Navigate to Build, Execution, Deployment>Kubernetes.
   - Click the + button to add a Kubernetes configuration.
   - Specify the Kubernetes API server endpoint and authentication details.
3. **Using Kubernetes in IntelliJ IDEA**:
   - Open the Kubernetes tool window (View>Tool Windows>Kubernetes).
   - Manage Kubernetes clusters, deployments, and services directly from the IDE.

Working with Cloud Services

IntelliJ IDEA can integrate with various cloud services, such as AWS, Google Cloud Platform (GCP), and Microsoft Azure, providing tools and plugins for managing cloud resources.

AWS Integration

1. **Install the AWS Toolkit Plugin**:
   - Go to the Plugins section in the settings and install the AWS Toolkit plugin.
2. **Configure AWS Credentials**:
   - Open the AWS tool window (View>Tool Windows>AWS Explorer).
   - Click Add Connection and provide your AWS credentials.

3. **Using AWS Services**:
   - ○ Manage AWS services like EC2, S3, Lambda, and more directly from the IDE.

Google Cloud Platform Integration

1. **Install the Google Cloud Tools Plugin**:
   - ○ Go to the Plugins section in the settings and install the Google Cloud Tools plugin.
2. **Configure GCP Credentials**:
   - ○ Open the Google Cloud tool window (View>Tool Windows>Google Cloud).
   - ○ Click Add Account and provide your GCP credentials.
3. **Using GCP Services**:
   - ○ Manage GCP services like Compute Engine, App Engine, Cloud Storage, and more directly from the IDE.

Microsoft Azure Integration

1. **Install the Azure Toolkit for IntelliJ Plugin**:
   - ○ Go to the Plugins section in the settings and install the Azure Toolkit for IntelliJ plugin.
2. **Configure Azure Credentials**:
   - ○ Open the Azure tool window (View>Tool Windows>Azure Explorer).
   - ○ Click Sign In and provide your Azure credentials.
3. **Using Azure Services**:
   - ○ Manage Azure services like Virtual Machines, App Services, Blob Storage, and more directly from the IDE.

7.3 Using the Database Tools

IntelliJ IDEA includes powerful database tools that allow you to connect to databases, run queries, and manage data directly from the IDE.

Database Tool Window

The Database tool window provides a comprehensive interface for working with databases.

Opening the Database Tool Window

1. **View Menu**:
   - Go to View>Tool Windows>Database.
2. **Toolbar Icon**:
   - Click the Database icon in the toolbar.

Configuring Database Connections

Setting up database connections in IntelliJ IDEA is straightforward and supports various database systems like MySQL, PostgreSQL, Oracle, and more.

Adding a Database Connection

1. **Open the Database Tool Window**:
   - Access the Database tool window as described above.
2. **Add a New Data Source**:
   - Click the + button and select Data Source><Database Type> (e.g., MySQL, PostgreSQL).
3. **Configure Connection Settings**:
   - Provide the necessary connection details, such as the database URL, username, and password.
   - Click Test Connection to verify the connection settings.
   - Click OK to save the connection.

Executing SQL Queries

IntelliJ IDEA provides a robust SQL editor for writing and executing queries.

Writing and Running Queries

1. **Open the SQL Console**:
   - Right-click the database connection in the Database tool window and select SQL Console.

149

2. **Write SQL Queries**:
   - o Use the SQL editor to write your queries.
   - o IntelliJ IDEA provides syntax highlighting, code completion, and error checking for SQL.
3. **Execute Queries**:
   - o Click the Run button in the SQL editor toolbar or press Ctrl + Enter (Windows/Linux) or Cmd + Enter (macOS) to execute the query.
   - o View the query results in the Results tab.

7.4 Customizing Keymaps and Macros

Customizing keymaps and macros in IntelliJ IDEA can significantly enhance your productivity by allowing you to streamline common tasks and create custom shortcuts.

Keymap Configuration

The keymap settings allow you to customize keyboard shortcuts for various actions in IntelliJ IDEA.

Configuring Keymaps

1. **Open the Settings/Preferences Dialog**:
   - o Go to File > Settings (Windows/Linux) or IntelliJ IDEA > Preferences (macOS).
2. **Navigate to Keymap**:
   - o Select Keymap from the left-hand menu.
3. **Customize Shortcuts**:
   - o Find the action you want to customize using the search bar or the list of actions.
   - o Right-click the action and select Add Keyboard Shortcut.
   - o Press the desired key combination and click OK.

Recording and Using Macros

Macros in IntelliJ IDEA allow you to record a sequence of actions and replay them with a single command.

Recording a Macro

1. **Start Recording**:
   - Go to Edit>Macros>Start Macro Recording.
2. **Perform Actions**:
   - Perform the sequence of actions you want to record.
3. **Stop Recording**:
   - Go to Edit>Macros>Stop Macro Recording.
   - Name the macro and save it.

Using Macros

1. **Execute a Macro**:
   - Go to Edit>Macros>Play <Macro Name>.
2. **Assign a Shortcut to a Macro**:
   - Open the Keymap settings.
   - Find the macro under Macros and assign a keyboard shortcut.

Custom Actions and Shortcuts

IntelliJ IDEA allows you to create custom actions and shortcuts to automate repetitive tasks.

Creating Custom Actions

1. **Use the Action Manager**:
   - Go to File>Settings (Windows/Linux) or IntelliJ IDEA>Preferences (macOS).
   - Navigate to Plugins and install the Action Manager plugin if not already installed.
2. **Define Custom Actions**:
   - Open the Action Manager tool window.
   - Create new actions by specifying the sequence of steps and assigning them a name.
3. **Assign Shortcuts to Custom Actions**:
   - Open the Keymap settings.

- Find the custom action under Plugins>Action Manager and assign a keyboard shortcut.

7.5 Using Live Templates

Live templates in IntelliJ IDEA allow you to create code snippets that can be inserted into your code with a simple abbreviation.

Creating Live Templates

1. **Open the Settings/Preferences Dialog**:
   - Go to File>Settings (Windows/Linux) or IntelliJ IDEA>Preferences (macOS).
2. **Navigate to Live Templates**:
   - Select Editor>Live Templates.
3. **Add a New Template**:
   - Click the + button to add a new live template.
   - Define the abbreviation, template text, and context where the template can be used.

Example: Creating a Live Template for a Java Method

1. **Add a New Template**:
   - Abbreviation: psvm
   - Template Text:

   ```java
   Copy code
   public static void main(String[] args) {
       $END$
   }
   ```

   - Context: Java

Managing and Organizing Templates

Live templates can be organized into groups and managed for better usability.

1. **Create Groups**:

- o In the Live Templates settings, click the + button and select Template Group.
- o Name the group (e.g., Java, SQL, HTML).

2. **Move Templates to Groups**:
    - o Drag and drop templates into the desired groups for better organization.

Sharing Templates with Team

Sharing live templates with your team ensures consistency and productivity across the development team.

Exporting Templates

1. **Export to File**:
    - o In the Live Templates settings, select the templates or groups you want to export.
    - o Click the Export button and save the templates to a file.

Importing Templates

1. **Import from File**:
    - o In the Live Templates settings, click the Import button.
    - o Select the file containing the live templates and import them into IntelliJ IDEA.

By mastering the advanced features and plugins in IntelliJ IDEA, you can significantly enhance your development workflow. From integrating third-party tools and using the powerful database tools to customizing keymaps and macros and leveraging live templates, this chapter provides comprehensive insights and practical steps to maximize your productivity and efficiency.

Chapter 8: Performance Tuning

IntelliJ IDEA is a powerful IDE that offers extensive features and capabilities. However, like any complex software, it can sometimes experience performance issues. This chapter will guide you through various techniques and best practices to optimize the performance of IntelliJ IDEA, ensuring a smooth and efficient development experience. We will cover optimizing IDE performance, managing memory usage, configuring JVM options, and speeding up build times.

8.1 Optimizing IDE Performance

Optimizing the performance of IntelliJ IDEA involves several strategies, including configuring memory settings, disabling unused plugins, and using performance profiling tools.

Configuring Memory Settings

Memory settings play a crucial role in the performance of IntelliJ IDEA. Allocating appropriate memory to the IDE can prevent sluggishness and crashes.

Adjusting the Heap Size

1. **Locate the idea.vmoptions File**:
   - The idea.vmoptions file contains JVM options, including memory settings.
   - On Windows, the file is located at
     C:\Users\<YourUserName>\.IntelliJIdea<Version>\config\idea64.exe.vmoptions.
   - On macOS, the file is located at
     /Users/<YourUserName>/Library/Preferences/IntelliJIdea<Version>/idea.vmoptions.
   - On Linux, the file is located at ~/.IntelliJIdea<Version>/config/idea64.vmoptions.
2. **Edit the File**:
   - Open the idea.vmoptions file in a text editor.
   - Adjust the -Xms (initial heap size) and -Xmx (maximum heap size) parameters.
   - Example configuration:

```
diff
Copy code
-Xms512m
-Xmx2048m
```

3. **Restart IntelliJ IDEA**:
   o Restart the IDE to apply the new memory settings.

Configuring Code Cache Size

1. **Edit the idea.vmoptions File**:
   o Add or modify the -XX:ReservedCodeCacheSize parameter.
   o Example configuration:

```
diff
Copy code
-XX:ReservedCodeCacheSize=512m
```

2. **Restart IntelliJ IDEA**:
   o Restart the IDE to apply the new code cache size setting.

Disabling Unused Plugins

Unused plugins can consume resources and slow down IntelliJ IDEA. Disabling unnecessary plugins can improve performance.

1. **Open the Settings/Preferences Dialog**:
   o Go to File > Settings (Windows/Linux) or IntelliJ IDEA > Preferences (macOS).
2. **Navigate to Plugins**:
   o Select Plugins from the left-hand menu.
3. **Disable Unused Plugins**:
   o In the Installed tab, uncheck the plugins you do not use.
   o Restart IntelliJ IDEA to apply the changes.

Performance Profiling Tools

IntelliJ IDEA includes tools to profile and monitor its performance, helping you identify and address bottlenecks.

CPU and Memory Profiler

1. **Open the Profiler**:
   o Go to Help>Diagnostic Tools>CPU and Memory Profiler.
2. **Start Profiling**:
   o Click Start CPU Usage Profiling or Start Memory Usage Profiling.
3. **Analyze Results**:
   o After collecting sufficient data, click Stop Profiling.
   o Analyze the profiling results to identify performance issues.

8.2 Managing Memory Usage

Understanding and managing memory usage is crucial for maintaining the performance of IntelliJ IDEA. This section covers understanding IDE memory usage, configuring garbage collection settings, and detecting memory leaks.

Understanding IDE Memory Usage

IntelliJ IDEA provides tools to monitor and analyze its memory usage, helping you identify and address memory-related issues.

Memory Indicator

1. **Enable Memory Indicator**:
   o Go to File>Settings (Windows/Linux) or IntelliJ IDEA>Preferences (macOS).
   o Navigate to Appearance & Behavior>Appearance.
   o Check Show memory indicator.
2. **Monitor Memory Usage**:
   o The memory indicator appears in the bottom-right corner of the IDE.
   o It shows the current memory usage and allows you to perform garbage collection by clicking on it.

Garbage Collection Settings

Garbage collection (GC) settings can significantly impact the performance of IntelliJ IDEA. Configuring GC settings can help manage memory usage more efficiently.

Configuring GC Parameters

1. **Edit the idea.vmoptions File**:
   - Add or modify GC-related parameters.
   - Example configuration:

   ```ruby
   ruby
   Copy code
   -XX:+UseG1GC
   -XX:InitiatingHeapOccupancyPercent=35
   -XX:+UseStringDeduplication
   ```

2. **Restart IntelliJ IDEA**:
   - Restart the IDE to apply the new GC settings.

Memory Leak Detection

Memory leaks can degrade performance and lead to crashes. IntelliJ IDEA provides tools to detect and address memory leaks.

Using the Memory Profiler

1. **Open the Profiler**:
   - Go to Help > Diagnostic Tools > Memory Profiler.
2. **Analyze Memory Usage**:
   - Click Capture Memory Snapshot to take a snapshot of the current memory usage.
   - Analyze the snapshot to identify objects that are consuming excessive memory.
3. **Identify and Fix Memory Leaks**:
   - Use the information from the memory snapshot to identify and fix memory leaks in your code.

8.3 Configuring JVM Options

Configuring JVM options can significantly impact the performance of IntelliJ IDEA. This section covers editing JVM options, understanding their performance impact, and best practices for JVM configuration.

Editing JVM Options

The idea.vmoptions file contains various JVM options that control the behavior and performance of IntelliJ IDEA.

Locating and Editing the idea.vmoptions File

1. **Locate the File**:
    o On Windows:

       C:\Users\<YourUserName>\.IntelliJIdea<Version>\config\idea64.exe.vmoptions.

    o On macOS:

       /Users/<YourUserName>/Library/Preferences/IntelliJIdea<Version>/idea.vmoptions.

    o On Linux: ~/.IntelliJIdea<Version>/config/idea64.vmoptions.

2. **Edit the File**:
    o Open the file in a text editor and add or modify JVM options.
    o Example options:

       ```diff
       Copy code
       -Xms512m
       -Xmx2048m
       -XX:+UseG1GC
       -XX:ReservedCodeCacheSize=512m
       ```

3. **Restart IntelliJ IDEA**:
    o Restart the IDE to apply the new JVM options.

Performance Impact of JVM Options

Understanding the performance impact of various JVM options can help you configure IntelliJ IDEA for optimal performance.

Key JVM Options

1. **Heap Size Options (-Xms, -Xmx)**:
    - These options control the initial and maximum heap size of the JVM.
    - Larger heap sizes can improve performance by reducing the frequency of garbage collection but require more memory.
2. **Garbage Collection Options (-XX:+UseG1GC, -XX:InitiatingHeapOccupancyPercent)**:
    - These options control the behavior of the garbage collector.
    - The G1 garbage collector (-XX:+UseG1GC) is recommended for its performance and efficiency.
3. **Code Cache Size (-XX:ReservedCodeCacheSize)**:
    - This option controls the size of the code cache.
    - Increasing the code cache size can improve performance by reducing the need to reload classes.

Best Practices for JVM Configuration

Following best practices for JVM configuration can help ensure optimal performance of IntelliJ IDEA.

Recommended JVM Options

1. **Heap Size**:
    - Set the heap size (-Xms, -Xmx) based on the available system memory and the size of your projects.
    - Example: -Xms512m -Xmx2048m.
2. **Garbage Collection**:
    - Use the G1 garbage collector (-XX:+UseG1GC) for its balance of performance and efficiency.
    - Configure additional GC options for better performance:

    ```ruby
    Copy code
    -XX:InitiatingHeapOccupancyPercent=35
    -XX:+UseStringDeduplication
    ```

3. **Code Cache**:
    - Increase the code cache size for large projects:

```diff
diff
Copy code
-XX:ReservedCodeCacheSize=512m
```

4. **Other Optimizations**:
   - Enable JVM optimizations for better performance:

```ruby
ruby
Copy code
-XX:+UseCompressedOops
-XX:+OptimizeStringConcat
```

8.4 Speeding Up Build Times

Build times can significantly impact your development workflow. This section covers techniques to speed up build times, including parallel builds, incremental compilation, and profiling build performance.

Parallel Builds

Parallel builds can significantly reduce build times by utilizing multiple CPU cores to compile your project.

Enabling Parallel Builds

1. **Open the Settings/Preferences Dialog**:
   - Go to File > Settings (Windows/Linux) or IntelliJ IDEA > Preferences (macOS).
2. **Navigate to Build Tools**:
   - Select Build, Execution, Deployment > Compiler.
3. **Enable Parallel Compilation**:
   - Check Compile independent modules in parallel.

Incremental Compilation

Incremental compilation compiles only the changes made since the last build, reducing build times.

Configuring Incremental Compilation

1. **Open the Settings/Preferences Dialog**:
    o Go to File>Settings (Windows/Linux) or IntelliJ IDEA>Preferences (macOS).
2. **Navigate to Compiler Settings**:
    o Select Build, Execution, Deployment>Compiler.
3. **Enable Incremental Compilation**:
    o Check Use "Build" tool window for building projects.

Profiling Build Performance

Profiling build performance can help identify bottlenecks and optimize build times.

Using Build Performance Profiler

1. **Enable Build Performance Profiler**:
    o Add the following JVM option to the idea.vmoptions file:

    ```lua
    lua
    Copy code
    -Didea.build.debug.logging=true
    ```

2. **Analyze Build Logs**:
    o Build your project and analyze the build logs for performance issues.
3. **Optimize Build Configuration**:
    o Use the insights from the build logs to optimize your build configuration, such as adjusting compiler settings and dependencies.

By following the techniques and best practices outlined in this chapter, you can optimize the performance of IntelliJ IDEA, ensuring a smooth and efficient development experience. From configuring memory settings and JVM options to managing memory usage and speeding up build times, these strategies will help you get the most out of your IDE.

Chapter 9: Collaboration and Teamwork

Collaboration and teamwork are essential components of modern software development. IntelliJ IDEA offers a variety of tools and features designed to enhance collaborative workflows and facilitate seamless integration with version control systems and code review tools. This chapter covers code collaboration tools, working with Git and GitHub, using code reviews, pair programming, and managing shared resources in IntelliJ IDEA.

9.1 Code Collaboration Tools

Effective code collaboration tools are crucial for teams working on the same project. IntelliJ IDEA provides built-in features and plugins to support real-time collaboration.

Code With Me

Code With Me is a powerful collaboration tool integrated into IntelliJ IDEA, allowing multiple developers to work on the same codebase simultaneously.

Setting Up Code With Me

1. **Starting a Session**:
   - Go to Tools>Code With Me>Start Session.
   - Select the access level for participants (Read-Only, Edit Files, Full Access).
2. **Inviting Participants**:
   - Share the session link with team members.
   - Participants can join using the link in their IntelliJ IDEA.
3. **Collaborating in Real-Time**:
   - Collaborate on code, share the terminal, and run/debug applications together.
   - Use the built-in chat and video call features for communication.

Using Collaboration Plugins

IntelliJ IDEA supports various plugins to enhance collaboration, such as Slack and Microsoft Teams integration.

Installing Collaboration Plugins

1. **Open the Plugins Dialog**:
   - Go to File > Settings (Windows/Linux) or IntelliJ IDEA > Preferences (macOS).
   - Select Plugins from the left-hand menu.
2. **Search and Install**:
   - Search for the desired plugin (e.g., Slack, Microsoft Teams).
   - Click Install and restart IntelliJ IDEA.

Configuring and Using Plugins

1. **Configuring Plugins**:
   - Go to File > Settings (Windows/Linux) or IntelliJ IDEA > Preferences (macOS).
   - Navigate to the plugin settings and configure them according to your needs.
2. **Using Plugins**:
   - Use the plugin to send notifications, share code snippets, and stay updated on project activities directly from IntelliJ IDEA.

Real-Time Code Sharing

Real-time code sharing allows developers to share code snippets and files instantly with team members.

Using Code With Me for Code Sharing

1. **Select Code to Share**:
   - Highlight the code snippet or file you want to share.
2. **Share via Code With Me**:
   - Right-click and select Share via Code With Me.
   - Choose the participants or generate a shareable link.
3. **Access Shared Code**:
   - Participants can view and edit the shared code in real-time.

9.2 Working with Git and GitHub

Git and GitHub integration are essential for version control and collaboration. IntelliJ IDEA provides robust Git support with various features for both basic and advanced operations.

Git Integration Basics

Setting Up Git in IntelliJ IDEA

1. **Install Git**:
   - o Ensure Git is installed on your system. Download it from git-scm.com.
2. **Configure Git in IntelliJ IDEA**:
   - o Go to File>Settings (Windows/Linux) or IntelliJ IDEA>Preferences (macOS).
   - o Navigate to Version Control>Git.
   - o Specify the path to the Git executable.

Basic Git Operations

1. **Cloning a Repository**:
   - o Go to VCS>Get from Version Control.
   - o Enter the repository URL and select a directory to clone the repository.
2. **Committing Changes**:
   - o Make changes to your code.
   - o Go to VCS>Commit or use the Commit button in the toolbar.
   - o Enter a commit message and click Commit.
3. **Pushing Changes**:
   - o After committing, go to VCS>Git>Push.
   - o Select the branch and click Push.

Advanced Git Operations

Branching and Merging

1. **Creating a Branch**:
   - o Go to VCS>Git>Branches.
   - o Click New Branch and enter a branch name.
2. **Switching Branches**:
   - o Go to VCS>Git>Branches.
   - o Select the branch you want to switch to.

3. **Merging Branches**:
   - Go to VCS > Git > Branches.
   - Select Merge into Current and choose the branch to merge.

Resolving Conflicts

1. **Identifying Conflicts**:
   - Conflicts occur during merging or rebasing when changes overlap.
   - IntelliJ IDEA highlights conflicting files.
2. **Resolving Conflicts**:
   - Open the conflicting file.
   - Use the merge tool provided by IntelliJ IDEA to resolve conflicts.
   - Mark the file as resolved.

Pull Requests and Code Reviews

Creating a Pull Request

1. **Push Your Branch**:
   - Ensure your branch is pushed to GitHub.
2. **Create a Pull Request on GitHub**:
   - Go to your repository on GitHub.
   - Click New pull request and select the branches to compare.
   - Enter a

title and description for the pull request, then click Create pull request.

3. **View and Manage Pull Requests in IntelliJ IDEA**:
   - Go to VCS > Git > GitHub.
   - Use the Pull Requests tab to view, create, and manage pull requests directly from IntelliJ IDEA.

Conducting Code Reviews

1. **Assign Reviewers**:
   - When creating a pull request, assign team members as reviewers.
2. **Review Code Changes**:

o   Reviewers can view changes, comment on specific lines, and suggest improvements.

3. **Merging Pull Requests**:

o   Once approved, merge the pull request on GitHub or directly from IntelliJ IDEA.

9.3 Using Code Reviews

Code reviews are essential for maintaining code quality and ensuring collaborative development. IntelliJ IDEA integrates with popular code review tools and provides built-in features to streamline the process.

Setting Up Code Reviews

Configuring Code Review Tools

1. **Integrate with GitHub or GitLab**:

o   Go to File>Settings (Windows/Linux) or IntelliJ IDEA>Preferences (macOS).

o   Navigate to Version Control>GitHub or GitLab.

o   Authenticate and configure your repository settings.

2. **Enable Code Review Plugins**:

o   Search for and install plugins like CodeStream or UpSource from the plugin repository.

o   Configure the plugin settings according to your team's requirements.

Reviewing Code Changes

Using the Pull Requests Tool Window

1. **Open the Pull Requests Tool Window**:

o   Go to View>Tool Windows>Pull Requests.

2. **Review Changes**:

o   Select a pull request to review.

o   View file changes, leave comments, and approve or request changes.

Inline Code Comments

1. **Adding Inline Comments**:

o   Highlight a specific line or block of code.

166

o Right-click and select Add Inline Comment.

2. **Viewing and Responding to Comments**:
   o View comments in the code editor.
   o Respond to comments directly within IntelliJ IDEA.

Integrating with Review Tools

1. **Connecting to Review Tools**:
   o Go to File>Settings (Windows/Linux) or IntelliJ IDEA>Preferences (macOS).
   o Navigate to the plugin settings for your review tool (e.g., CodeStream, UpSource).
2. **Reviewing Code**:
   o Use the review tool's features to manage and conduct reviews.
   o Access review dashboards, comment histories, and approvals.

9.4 Pair Programming with IntelliJ IDEA

Pair programming is a collaborative technique where two developers work together on the same codebase. IntelliJ IDEA supports pair programming through various tools and practices.

Pair Programming Techniques

Driver-Navigator Model

1. **Driver**:
   o The driver writes the code and focuses on the implementation details.
2. **Navigator**:
   o The navigator reviews each line of code as it is written, providing feedback and suggestions.

Setting Up Collaborative Sessions

Using Code With Me for Pair Programming

1. **Start a Session**:
   o Go to Tools>Code With Me>Start Session.
   o Select the access level for the navigator.

2. **Invite the Navigator**:
   - o Share the session link with your pair programming partner.
3. **Collaborate in Real-Time**:
   - o Work on the codebase together, share ideas, and implement solutions in real-time.

Using Screen Sharing Tools

1. **Choose a Screen Sharing Tool**:
   - o Use tools like Zoom, Microsoft Teams, or Google Meet for screen sharing.
2. **Start a Session**:
   - o Share your screen and IDE with your pair programming partner.
3. **Collaborate**:
   - o Discuss and write code together, with one person sharing their screen while the other provides feedback.

Best Practices for Pair Programming

1. **Switch Roles Regularly**:
   - o Alternate between the driver and navigator roles to keep both participants engaged.
2. **Communicate Effectively**:
   - o Maintain clear and open communication to ensure a productive session.
3. **Use Short Iterations**:
   - o Work in short, focused iterations to maintain momentum and avoid fatigue.

9.5 Managing Shared Resources

Managing shared resources ensures consistency and efficiency across development teams. IntelliJ IDEA provides tools for sharing code styles, project templates, and libraries.

Shared Code Styles

Configuring Code Styles

1. **Open Code Style Settings**:

- o Go to File>Settings (Windows/Linux) or IntelliJ IDEA>Preferences (macOS).
- o Navigate to Editor>Code Style.
2. **Configure Code Style**:
   - o Set code formatting rules, indentation, and other style settings.

Exporting and Importing Code Styles

1. **Export Code Style**:
   - o Go to Editor>Code Style.
   - o Click Manage and select Export.
2. **Import Code Style**:
   - o Go to Editor>Code Style.
   - o Click Manage and select Import.
3. **Share Code Style Files**:
   - o Share the exported code style file with your team.
   - o Import the shared file into each team member's IntelliJ IDEA.

Project Templates

Creating Project Templates

1. **Set Up a Base Project**:
   - o Create a new project with the desired configurations and settings.
2. **Save as Template**:
   - o Go to File>Save Project as Template.
3. **Name and Save the Template**:
   - o Provide a name and description for the template, then save it.

Using Project Templates

1. **Create a New Project from Template**:
   - o Go to File>New Project.
   - o Select Project from Template and choose your saved template.
2. **Customize the New Project**:
   - o Customize the new project as needed.

Shared Libraries and Frameworks

Configuring Shared Libraries

1. **Add Library to Project**:
   - Go to File>Project Structure>Libraries.
   - Add the desired libraries to your project.
2. **Export Library Configuration**:
   - Export the library configuration file from the project settings.
3. **Import Library Configuration**:
   - Share the configuration file with your team.
   - Import the shared file into each team member's IntelliJ IDEA.

Using Frameworks

1. **Configure Frameworks**:
   - Go to File>Project Structure>Modules.
   - Add and configure the required frameworks for your project.
2. **Share Framework Configuration**:
   - Export the framework configuration file.
   - Share and import the configuration file as needed.

By effectively leveraging the collaboration and teamwork features in IntelliJ IDEA, development teams can enhance their productivity, maintain code quality, and streamline their workflows. Whether through real-time code sharing, robust Git integration, comprehensive code reviews, or pair programming sessions, IntelliJ IDEA provides a powerful platform for collaborative software development. Managing shared resources such as code styles, project templates, and libraries further ensures consistency and efficiency across the team.

Chapter 10: Mastering IntelliJ IDEA

IntelliJ IDEA is a powerful integrated development environment (IDE) that offers a vast array of features designed to enhance productivity and streamline the software development process. This chapter aims to help you master IntelliJ IDEA by exploring available learning resources, providing productivity tips and tricks, troubleshooting common issues, staying up-to-date with new features, and examining real-world case studies.

10.1 Learning Resources and Communities

To get the most out of IntelliJ IDEA, it's crucial to tap into the wealth of learning resources and communities available. These resources can help you deepen your understanding of the IDE, keep up with the latest updates, and connect with other users.

Official Documentation

The official documentation for IntelliJ IDEA is comprehensive and regularly updated, making it an essential resource for both beginners and advanced users.

Key Sections of the Documentation

1. **Getting Started**:
   - Introduction to IntelliJ IDEA.
   - Installation and initial setup guides.
2. **User Guide**:
   - Detailed explanations of features and functionalities.
   - Step-by-step tutorials for common tasks.
3. **Reference**:
   - Configuration settings.
   - Keyboard shortcuts and command references.
4. **API and Plugin Development**:
   - Information for developers looking to extend IntelliJ IDEA with plugins.

Accessing the Documentation

- **Online**: The official documentation is available on the JetBrains website at https://www.jetbrains.com/idea/documentation/.
- **In-IDE**: Access the documentation directly within IntelliJ IDEA via the Help menu.

Online Tutorials and Courses

Online tutorials and courses provide structured learning paths and practical examples to help you master IntelliJ IDEA.

Popular Online Platforms

1. **JetBrains Academy**:
   o Interactive courses created by JetBrains.
   o Includes courses on IntelliJ IDEA features and programming languages.
2. **Udemy**:
   o Offers a variety of courses on IntelliJ IDEA, ranging from beginner to advanced levels.
3. **Coursera**:
   o Provides courses from top universities and institutions, including IntelliJ IDEA training.
4. **YouTube**:
   o Numerous free tutorials and walkthroughs are available on YouTube channels dedicated to software development and IntelliJ IDEA.

Recommended Courses

- **IntelliJ IDEA Essentials**: Covers the basics of the IDE, including navigation, editing, and debugging.
- **Advanced IntelliJ IDEA**: Explores advanced features such as refactoring, code analysis, and customization.
- **Plugin Development for IntelliJ IDEA**: Teaches how to develop and integrate plugins into IntelliJ IDEA.

Community Forums and User Groups

Joining community forums and user groups can provide support, share knowledge, and network with other IntelliJ IDEA users.

Notable Forums and Groups

1. **JetBrains Community Forum**:
   o   Official forum for discussing IntelliJ IDEA.
   o   Categories for general discussion, troubleshooting, and feature requests.
2. **Stack Overflow**:
   o   Popular platform for asking questions and sharing knowledge.
   o   Use the intellij-idea tag to find relevant discussions and solutions.
3. **Reddit**:
   o   Subreddits like r/IntelliJIDEA and r/JetBrains are active communities for discussing the IDE and related topics.
4. **Meetup.com**:
   o   Look for local user groups and meetups focused on IntelliJ IDEA and JetBrains tools.

10.2 Tips and Tricks for Productivity

IntelliJ IDEA is packed with features designed to boost your productivity. This section explores essential keyboard shortcuts, hidden features, and daily workflow enhancements.

Keyboard Shortcuts and Commands

Mastering keyboard shortcuts can significantly speed up your workflow. Here are some essential shortcuts:

Basic Navigation

- **Go to Class/File/Symbol**:
   o   Ctrl+N (Windows/Linux) / Cmd+O (macOS): Open class.
   o   Ctrl+Shift+N (Windows/Linux) / Cmd+Shift+O (macOS): Open file.
   o   Ctrl+Alt+Shift+N (Windows/Linux) / Cmd+Option+O (macOS): Open symbol.
- **Recent Files**:
   o   Ctrl+E (Windows/Linux) / Cmd+E (macOS): Show recent files.
- **Navigate to Declaration**:
   o   Ctrl+B or Ctrl+Click (Windows/Linux) / Cmd+B or Cmd+Click (macOS): Navigate to declaration.

Editing

- **Basic Code Completion**:
    - Ctrl+Space (Windows/Linux) / Ctrl+Space (macOS): Trigger basic code completion.
- **Smart Code Completion**:
    - Ctrl+Shift+Space (Windows/Linux) / Ctrl+Shift+Space (macOS): Trigger smart code completion.
- **Reformat Code**:
    - Ctrl+Alt+L (Windows/Linux) / Cmd+Option+L (macOS): Reformat the code according to code style settings.

Refactoring

- **Rename**:
    - Shift+F6 (Windows/Linux) / Shift+F6 (macOS): Rename symbol.
- **Extract Method/Variable**:
    - Ctrl+Alt+M / Ctrl+Alt+V (Windows/Linux) / Cmd+Option+M / Cmd+Option+V (macOS): Extract method/variable.

Hidden Features and Easter Eggs

IntelliJ IDEA includes several hidden features and easter eggs that can enhance your development experience.

Hidden Features

1. **Advanced Search and Replace**:
    - Use regex in search and replace dialogs for powerful text manipulation.
    - Ctrl+R (Windows/Linux) / Cmd+R (macOS): Replace in file.
    - Ctrl+Shift+R (Windows/Linux) / Cmd+Shift+R (macOS): Replace in project.
2. **Multicursor Editing**:
    - Alt+Click (Windows/Linux) / Option+Click (macOS): Add multiple cursors for simultaneous editing.
3. **Scratch Files**:
    - Ctrl+Shift+Alt+Insert (Windows/Linux) / Cmd+Shift+Option+N (macOS): Create a scratch file for temporary notes or code snippets.

Easter Eggs

1. **Flight Simulator**:
   - o Enter the following in the search bar and press Enter: Help! I'm trapped in a fortune cookie factory!.
2. **ASCII Art**:
   - o In the terminal, type fortune | cowsay to display a fun message with ASCII art.

Daily Workflow Enhancements

Incorporating certain practices into your daily workflow can help you use IntelliJ IDEA more efficiently.

Customizing Your Layout

1. **Tool Windows**:
   - o Use Alt+Number (Windows/Linux) / Cmd+Number (macOS) to quickly open tool windows like Project, Terminal, and Version Control.
2. **Splitting Editor**:
   - o Split the editor horizontally or vertically using Ctrl+Alt+S (Windows/Linux) / Cmd+Option+S (macOS).

Leveraging Live Templates

1. **Create Custom Templates**:
   - o Go to File>Settings>Editor>Live Templates.
   - o Define new templates for frequently used code snippets.
2. **Using Predefined Templates**:
   - o Trigger live templates using the associated abbreviation and Tab.

10.3 Troubleshooting Common Issues

Even with its robust design, you may encounter issues while using IntelliJ IDEA. This section covers common error messages, debugging IDE issues, and reporting bugs.

Common Error Messages

Understanding common error messages can help you quickly resolve issues.

Common Errors

1. **Out of Memory Errors**:
   - o   Solution: Increase the IDE's memory allocation in idea.vmoptions.
2. **Project SDK Not Defined**:
   - o   Solution: Go to File>Project Structure>Project and define the SDK.
3. **Plugin Compatibility Issues**:
   - o   Solution: Ensure plugins are up-to-date and compatible with your IDE version.

Debugging IDE Issues

When encountering IDE-related problems, use the following steps to diagnose and resolve them.

Collecting Logs

1. **Enable Debug Logging**:
   - o   Go to Help>Diagnostic Tools>Debug Log Settings.
   - o   Add the relevant categories to capture detailed logs.
2. **View Logs**:
   - o   Go to Help>Show Log in Explorer (Windows/Linux) / Show Log in Finder (macOS).

Resetting IDE Settings

1. **Restore Default Settings**:
   - o   Go to File>Manage IDE Settings>Restore Default Settings.
2. **Invalidating Caches**:
   - o   Go to File>Invalidate Caches / Restart.

Reporting Bugs and Issues

If you encounter a bug, report it to the JetBrains team for resolution.

Reporting Bugs

1. **Submit a Bug Report**:
   - o   Go to Help>Submit a Bug Report.
   - o   Provide detailed information, including IDE version, operating system, and steps to reproduce the issue.
2. **Community Support**:

o   Post your issue on the JetBrains Community Forum or Stack Overflow for community assistance.

10.4 Keeping Up with Updates and New Features

Staying updated with the latest features and improvements in IntelliJ IDEA can enhance your development experience.

IDE Update Channels

IntelliJ IDEA offers various update channels to suit different needs.

Update Channels

1. **Stable Releases**:
    o   Regular updates with thoroughly tested features and fixes.
2. **EAP (Early Access Program)**:
    o   Access to the latest features and improvements before they are officially released.

Switching Update Channels

1. **Change Update Channel**:
    o   Go to File > Settings > Appearance & Behavior > System Settings > Updates.
    o   Select the desired update channel (Stable, Beta, EAP).

Previewing New Features

Explore and test new features before they are officially released.

Participating in EAP

1. **Join EAP**:
    o   Sign up for the Early Access Program on the JetBrains website.
2. **Install EAP Builds**:
    o   Download and install EAP builds to access new features and provide feedback.

Participating in EAP (Early Access Program)

The Early Access Program (EAP) allows you to try out new features and improvements in IntelliJ IDEA before they are officially released.

Benefits of EAP

1. **Early Access**:
   o Be the first to try new features and improvements.
2. **Feedback**:
   o Provide feedback to help shape the development of IntelliJ IDEA.
3. **Community Involvement**:
   o Engage with the JetBrains community and developers.

Joining EAP

1. **Sign Up for EAP**:
   o Visit the JetBrains website and sign up for the EAP.
2. **Install EAP Builds**:
   o Download and install EAP builds from the JetBrains website or within IntelliJ IDEA.

10.5 Case Studies and Real-World Examples

Learning from real-world examples and case studies can provide valuable insights into the practical applications of IntelliJ IDEA.

Success Stories from Developers

Explore success stories from developers who have effectively used IntelliJ IDEA to enhance their productivity and achieve their goals.

Case Study: Acme Corp

Background: Acme Corp, a leading software development company, adopted IntelliJ IDEA to improve their development process.

Challenges:

- Fragmented development environment.
- Inefficient code review process.

- Difficulty managing large codebases.

Solutions:

1. **Unified Development Environment**:
   - Standardized on IntelliJ IDEA across all teams.
   - Improved collaboration and consistency.
2. **Streamlined Code Reviews**:
   - Integrated code review tools within IntelliJ IDEA.
   - Enhanced code quality and reduced review times.
3. **Efficient Code Management**:
   - Leveraged IntelliJ IDEA's powerful navigation and refactoring tools.
   - Improved code maintainability and reduced technical debt.

Results:

- Increased developer productivity by 30%.
- Improved code quality and reduced bugs.
- Enhanced team collaboration and satisfaction.

Practical Applications of IntelliJ IDEA

Explore practical applications of IntelliJ IDEA in various development scenarios.

Application Development

1. **Web Development**:
   - Use IntelliJ IDEA's built-in support for JavaScript, TypeScript, and popular frameworks like React and Angular.
   - Leverage tools like the integrated terminal, version control, and debugging features.
2. **Mobile Development**:
   - Develop Android applications using IntelliJ IDEA's Android support.
   - Integrate with the Android SDK and use features like code completion, debugging, and emulation.

Automation and Scripting

1. **Build Automation**:

- o Configure and manage build tools like Maven and Gradle.
- o Automate build processes and dependency management.

2. **Scripting**:
   - o Use IntelliJ IDEA's support for scripting languages like Python, Ruby, and Groovy.
   - o Automate repetitive tasks and streamline workflows.

Lessons Learned from Real Projects

Learn from the experiences of other developers and teams who have successfully used IntelliJ IDEA in their projects.

Key Lessons

1. **Embrace IntelliJ IDEA's Features**:
   - o Take advantage of the powerful features and tools available in IntelliJ IDEA.
   - o Continuously explore and learn new features to stay productive.

2. **Customize Your Environment**:
   - o Customize IntelliJ IDEA to fit your workflow and preferences.
   - o Use plugins, themes, and settings to enhance your development experience.

3. **Stay Updated**:
   - o Keep up with updates and new features to leverage the latest improvements.
   - o Participate in the Early Access Program to stay ahead of the curve.

4. **Collaborate Effectively**:
   - o Use IntelliJ IDEA's collaboration tools to work efficiently with your team.
   - o Share resources, code styles, and project templates to ensure consistency.

By mastering IntelliJ IDEA, you can significantly enhance your productivity, streamline your development process, and achieve greater success in your projects. Whether through learning resources, productivity tips, troubleshooting techniques, or real-world examples, this chapter provides the knowledge and tools needed to become an IntelliJ IDEA expert.

www.ingramcontent.com/pod-product-compliance
Lightning Source LLC
Chambersburg PA
CBHW080530060326
40690CB00022B/5084